Management in the Twenty First Century

Management in the Twenty First Century
----*A primer*----

Joseph L. Dineen

toExcel
New York   San Jose   Lincoln   Shanghai

Management in the Twenty First Century
All Rights Reserved. Copyright ©1999 by Joseph L. Dineen

No part of this book may be reproduced or transmitted in any form or by any means, graphic, electronic, or mechanical, including photocopying, recording, taping, or by any information storage or retrieval system, without the permission in writing from the publisher.

This edition published by toExcel Press,
an imprint of iUniverse.com, Inc.

For information address:
iUniverse.com, Inc.
620 North 48th Street
Suite 201
Lincoln, NE 68504-3467
www.iUniverse.com

ISBN: 1-58348-701-8

CONTENTS

Preface vii

If I were my employee
would I follow me? 1

I know I can lead
but will they follow? 17

Why do I have such trouble
getting them to understand
What I want done? 33

How do my employees resemble
the characters on the right?
or when I say "right"
why do they invariably go "left"? 47

Wait 'till he gets in here!
I'll wring his neck!
or how can he be so stupid!
I've told him over and over and over! 59

Stress management
or they're driving me crazy!
What can I do? 77

Now that I know me and my employees,
how do I put them together as a team? 89

Here you are!
At the top of the heap!
The Boss! It's tough to get there!
Can you stay? 97

Bibliography 103

About the author 105

PREFACE

After almost thirty years of business management experience, including administrative, human resources, customer service, technical service as well as years of teaching basic management subjects to corporations and formal classes, the subject of management in the year 2000 and beyond becomes a mystery. This mystery, coming as it does on the wave of the informational highway, the changing values of the business and the businessperson, the ethical and governmental adjustments that we have undergone, raises a monumental question as to how I can be successful or, more important, how can I be happy in my work?

This book will attempt to point out the "flavor" of management for the next century based upon what we have learned from the past and what we anticipate in the future. We will deal with what we really want and what we do not seem to be getting from our work and how we can deal with this dilemma. In fact, why does our work tend not to give us the sense of "belonging, comradeship, being needed, or being part of a family."

To look into the future, we will try to understand the past and build on that. We will try to understand the nature of "getting a job" and what we should expect from an employer. More important, we will search for the management skills that will take us into the future as well as to handle our own personal needs from management. Finally, we will try to make this "work" ethic meaningful for our happiness and success.

Among other things, we are now in an era of economic instability, both domestically and in the international marketplace, that is unparalleled in our history. The '50s demonstrated an economic growth in the post war era that was also unparalleled. In addition, family values in the '50s remained at the core of our existence and management style.

True, it is not fashionable to consider the family unit as a basis for success in the '90s because those values that existed in the past are not considered, generally, to be valuable in the '90s. The stability that existed then is now shattered because of "upward mobility:, relocations, and the speed of travel that has allowed us to expand our business and interest far afield from the "core family" and, even, the "core home base of the business." As such, it is now a chore for us all to get back to our roots, come home for the holidays and greet the family unit because it is spread over many miles, states, and, perhaps, countries. Without that stability to build on, the central value system that had been established in the more agrarian days has disappeared and we are now more "modern" and flexible than we were before. Whether this is an asset or liability is for you to judge. The fact is that we do have to live in this environment and we had better come to understand its complexities so we can survive and be successful.

With these changes in mind, we find the same confusion, misunderstanding and disagreements, that we face in our own personal lives, exist in the business and work world. In this book, we will look at what these problems are and what we can do about them in the real world. Some of note are:

1. The corporation, despite the feelings of the social libertarians, is not a living, breathing, and caring "family unit."
2. The corporation has one identifiable goal. That goal is to make a profit, period. In the manufacture and sale of a product or service, in order to provide jobs and some security for people, the corporation must make more money than it spends. Done wisely, the profit return is then re-invested and more jobs are made available and

new products can be brought on line, more profits made, etc. etc.
3. If the corporation fails to make profits, then no jobs can be created and, worse still, the corporation might have to "downsize" in order to maintain the profit level, or come up with a new product without capital money, or go under. Sadly, the later is the route of the future if we are not able to come to terms with the definition of "profit" as not being a "four letter word."
4. Recognition that the corporation does not "owe the employee anything. When hired, an employee is asked to do a job for a salary. If the employee does the job well, he/she gets paid the agreed upon amount that was negotiated at hire. If the employee has some ideas that add to the value of the product and the profit margin, (remember that the corporation does not intrinsically owe the employee anything more than the original salary) the corporation could, and usually does, give raises, increase benefits, promotions, etc. if it chooses to do so. But it does not have to do that as an obligation. On the other hand, if the employee is dissatisfied with his/her treatment at this corporation, the choice still exists for them to leave and seek better treatment elsewhere. Why be unhappy either way?
5. Remember that all life is composed of choices. If a choice is made, then you live with the consequences of that choice or make another one. If you live with a bad choice, then you have made the decision and you have no right to conduct a campaign of bitterness or invective against the corporation or fellow employees. Why? Because you do have the right to make another choice to try to make things better for you.
6. History tends to repeat itself. This remark has proven to be true in many more cases than not. Therefore, in management, we need to understand the basics as to

what has happened in order to form a foundation for planning our new management style for the future. This book will combine the past with the future so you can have that foundation upon which to build.

This book is a primer. It is not intended as an academic tome written for experts. It is written for the supervisor, management and executive who wants to remember what can be successful for them, not for everyone else. Takes some of these ideas, remember what used to work well for you, and build your own management style for the year 2000 and beyond. The work done now will make the future easier for you and your employees.

IF I WERE MY EMPLOYEE, WOULD I FOLLOW ME?

The vocational change from that of a worker to one entailing management is a critical responsibility that you have assumed. Many times, your employer will send you to a seminar on how to supervise and that is all of the training that you will receive.

You have to rely on your experience and observations of others or mentors who are willing to help you understand how to lead.

Tom Peters in his book *Thriving on Chaos* demonstrates clearly that the only constant that you can count on is change. Therefore you are operating in a world of business that might not be the same twice or, even worse, that changes again right after you have corrected the problems from the last change. Vast amounts of material have been published on the subject of management. No practical review of the principles involved in management can be summarized in one book. However, in the era of chaos, there are several principles that are basic and will be discussed as they appear constantly in the literature on the subject.

Since you will probably continue in some form of management for the rest of your career, it is recommended that you look at the bibliography at the end of this book and look for some different ideas that might be used in the development of your personal style and character traits.

Acquiring knowledge of your corporation's business, functions, rules and regulations is very important for your success. However, your position now requires you to broaden your perspective and to study the raw material of management, people. People are the most complicated, sensitive and expensive equipment that you can manage as well as the corporation's most valuable asset. Some sociologists say that people intrinsically want to work. However, how well they work to accomplish the task at hand means that they have to be inspired and taught how to work efficiently. In other words, people must be channeled so they can reach their maximum potential for YOUR corporation.

Notice how that last sentence is worded. People, as you know, want to perform a job correctly. However, in your corporation, you have methods and procedures on how you want a job performed. With that in mind, your people should perform the job the way your corporation wants the job done, not the way they want it done. Herein lies the rub, as Shakespeare would say. How do you get people to do the job the way you want it done?

How do you do this without stifling individual initiative and creativity?

To effectively lead people, you must have some understanding as to what makes them "tick." Before you can begin this search, you must understand yourself, your characteristics, and your foundation for leadership. This next section will set some parameters for you to perform an evaluation on the most important person in this room now, YOU.

WHO AM I? CAN I LEAD?

In many ways, the following task is the most difficult management program that you will face because you need to evaluate *yourself in an honest and objective way* because the only one who will be deceived, if you fail to lay aside your personal defenses that everyone uses on a daily basis to minimize weaknesses and glorify strengths in themselves, is you.

Self appraisal requires courage to look at yourself and inventory weaknesses and strengths. BUT, more important, you must decide if you wish to take the effort to correct weaknesses, no matter what that effort takes. Even if you choose not to work on weaknesses, you will be better for the exercise because you will have recognized your weaknesses and be able to deal with them in the workplace as a leader. You owe yourself this effort in self-analysis, no matter how painful it may be to yourself. The benefit will be to you, your family, and your employees.

There is a self-evaluation form at the end of this section that may help you in this appraisal. It is set out as a list of characteristics, emotions, and goals. You should assess yourself by determining if each category is an asset or liability. Once done, determine WHY it is either and what you have to do about it to correct a weakness or expand on a strength.

Note that this list is not complete because you will, undoubtedly, be able to add items to the list that are important to you. Do not limit yourself in any way in performing this appraisal. The more comprehensive it is, the better your evaluation will be.

You will also note in using this list that you will have to define the subject yourself. Clever definitions and explanations have been avoided because it is assumed that you will be able to define every one of these terms as they pertain to the human personality in yourself and others.

It is easy for you to skip over this process without devoting the time and effort that it warrants. No one is keeping tabs on you. But if you do skim over it and proceed without thinking about yourself in the framework of building strong management skills, you and your employees will lose. The loss comes from not having that strong foundation that will let you build management skills as well as not being able to understand how to inspire your employees to do good work because you don't understand what makes you "tick."

Take the time now to begin doing good management work by understanding yourself.

SELF EVALUATION CHECKLIST

DEFINE AND REVIEW EACH CATEGORY, DETERMINE IF IT IS AN ASSET OR LIABILITY AND THEN DETERMINE WHY OR WHAT NEEDS TO BE DONE.

CHARACTERISTIC	ASSET LIABILITY	WHY?
Flexibility		
Ambition		
Cheerfulness		
Courage		
Courtesy		
Appearance		
Education		
Enthusiasm		
Belief in system		
Friendliness		
Graciousness		
Habits		
Health		
Imagination		
Integrity		
Intelligence		
Loyalty		
Memory		
Observation		
Open-mindedness		
Organization		
Perseverance		
Power of Expression		
Punctuality		
Reasoning		
Reputation		
Self Confidence		
Sincerity		

Tact	_____
Thoroughness	_____
Family values	_____
Voice	_____

Use additional sheets to address each issue in detail.

Once you have determined your own qualities, positive and negative, the next step is to evaluate some basic personality traits that are necessary for success now and in the future.

The list on the self evaluation sheet is very extensive, plus those areas that you have added. However, there are some of those traits that are more significant than others when good leadership, or management, is the goal. Of course, all of the traits are important. But if you place any emphasis on improvement, then some take precedence over others.

An effective leader must have the following traits or attitudes working for him/her to be successful:

1. Enthusiasm
2. Courage
3. Self Confidence
4. Integrity
5. Friendliness.

Enthusiasm is a necessary factor in the accomplishment of every worthwhile goal. Webster defines it as: "to be inspired... strong excitement of feeling." When we approach our own jobs with a less than "inspired" attitude, that attitude trickles down to most of the employees and they work with a poorer attitude. In fact, your employees tend to mirror your attitude toward the job. Therefore if you have personal problems, problems with the job, problems with a process or problems with employees or peers and reflect these problems in your approach to completing your job, your employees will follow track and produce less or not produce the quality product necessary to compete. Then, you react negatively and they respond more negatively. This continues in a downward spiral until poor work or process comes to the attention of your management and they react negatively etc., etc.

If it is the feeling in a company workday that what is being done is significant, both to you and your employees, all will contribute to the good of the corporation as well as to the good of the employee.

Enthusiasm is a spirit or climate that pervades a department and is perceptible to employees and visitors as well as other departments when they visit your area. It has also been defined as a climate of productivity; the attitude is "can do."

Does this mean that I cannot have a "bad day"? In the long run, you have to control your internal problems at all times and face your employees with that spirit that inspires them to good work. In effect, you are channeling creative energy into your people anticipating that it will produce a creative effort from them.

Some vehicles of enthusiasm are "team spirit," "esprit de corp," and the feeling that "the difficult we can do immediately, only the impossible takes a little longer."

If you do not feel enthusiastic about your job, the function of your department, the management and the company itself, you will not be able to carry this attitude to your employees. If you don't have it and want it, analyze yourself and determine the reasons so you can concentrate on improving. If you don't have it and don't want it because you do not feel enthusiastic about some element of your job, leave. Why should you, the company and your employees be miserable?

Courage is defined as "the mental or moral strength to venture, persevere or withstand danger, fear or difficulty." A more limited definition is "the ability to react to adversity by coming back harder than ever."

Some have said that when nothing goes wrong, nothing is being done. Courage is not called upon when nothing is happening or when everything is going right. But when things start to go wrong, it is critical to the success of the operation. Without it, the product, project or even the company could fail or, at least, lack accomplishment and lose marketshare or become less competitive.

Sometimes, courage is required to just come to work because you know that you are faced with a problem that must be dealt with today. This causes headaches, stomach aches or worse because, generally, we must deal with this problem through brainpower and not manpower. Not only must we think of solutions but we must also be able to persuade and direct that solution to completion. This courage requires stamina, knowledge, grit, and guts. And we are only dealing with people and products. What if it was more serious, like a life or death situation?

You need this reservoir of courage almost every working day because things go wrong almost every day and you have to fix it.

If you feel that this requirement is more than you can stand, management is not a vocation that you should pursue. Theodore Roosevelt was aware of the fact that actions and feelings are closely related. His formula for success was that when courage seemed to be failing him, he acted as if he were courageous because he then felt more courageous. This formula can stand up well today and will continue to bear fruit in the next century.

The old NFL standby saying is that you win games through good defense. However, in the marketplace, most games are won because you have scored more points than your opponent. In other words, the aggressive offense is the best defense. The package of success is effectively combining the traits of enthusiasm, courage and self confidence in both the coaches and players.

Self Confidence is not arrogance, conceit or snobbishness. Having done your self analysis, you know yourself, your accomplishments, your skills, and the areas noted for improvement. Having identified what you do well, this knowledge acts as a bolstering quality that helps you to overcome any feelings of inferiority that you may have.

If you can see your level of self confidence AND identify the level in your employees, they will prove real added value to your organization when you leave theirs and yours intact. If you degrade or challenge to a fault your employee's self confidence, you can destroy it an impair the very functions that you manage. Build on their strengths instead of weaknesses. Tie criticisms or suggestions into reminders of how much better an employee can perform. Thus you build an employee towards reaching his/her potential as well as support your management position because you will also be successful if they are successful.

Self confidence is the knowledge that you can get the job done and that you can face and overcome obstacles in your path in order to accomplish that goal.

Integrity, or honesty, is the adherence to a code of moral values and ethics. You should have loyalties and responsibilities to your corporation, your peers, your subordinates, the public, and, most important, to your family. This set of values basically says that you have and will continue to do the "right" thing by them. This understanding by them, because you have done this in the past, is that they trust you to continue to perform in that way. As a manager, you cannot afford to be less than honest in any dealings with your employees. Because once you have failed in this way, it is virtually impossible to regain your former stature with any of the above.

Unfortunately, we do not live in a perfect world. The real world is full of lies and deceit. So, how can I adhere to this strict code that you mention when the real world calls for me to be less than honest, at times?

Without getting into a lengthily discussion of business ethics and the real world, let's say that your employees are looking at you for integrity. You do have a choice, to be honest or not.

Being honest does not mean that you tell your employees everything and answer every question that is asked. Every employee knows that there are business discussions that they are not privileged to know. (They may want to know but they understand that the timing may not be right for them to know now.) It does not violate a code of values to say "I am not at liberty to discuss that right now" or "I really don't know" rather than to construct a story that might call into question your honesty at a later date.

If you are called upon to lie by someone, remember that you do have a choice and each choice has risks associated with the decision. However, you need to do what is right for you and your code of moral conduct as it relates to your corporation, your peers, your employees, the public, and, most important, your family. Choose wisely and choose well!

Remember what your integrity means to you and your employees when you do choose.

Friendliness involves expressing a sincere interest in and warm regard for an individual. In the work environment, it cannot be counterfeited with insincere comments or actions or the appearance of listening to an employee when your mind is a hundred miles away. However, it also does not involve giving our hugs and plaudits when they are not earned or when perceived to be false.

True friendliness depends upon your personality and that of your employee, as well as other factors. The important point is that the employee wants to know that his/her manager really knows him and is interested in his success, even if it only with the company and not on a personal level. The value to the relationship is added when the manager lets the employee know that opinions, interests, and family are important to both as well as that the manager "approves" of the employee as a person. This is a "value added" relationship.

Getting too friendly or too remote are both equally dangerous to a manager-employee relationship. Therefore this is a fine line that is walked by all in management. Which way is correct? The one that fits the situation, the people and the corporate goals. Once you determine that, your road is somewhat easier but not much.

Now that you have looked inside yourself and determined that you not only have the basic character traits and interests to be a good manager but you also want to continue your career in that regard, the next step is to look at your employees as human beings and try to figure out what makes them "tick" and how can I get them to do the job.

WHAT DO MY EMPLOYEES *NEED* SO THEY CAN DO THE JOB WELL?

Psychologists and sociologists have long looked at human behavior to determine what makes people do what they do. Basically, they have looked for the essential requirements for survival. They have interpreted needs as to what an individual must have and what is wanted. Unfortunately, while this is addresses as "science," people do the strangest things. Therefore many theories exist and many books have been written about human needs.

Combining many of the theories produces some generic results as to human need. They are so obvious when we look at them in others that we tend to ignore that they exist in ourselves as well.

For example, in order to survive, we need food, drink, shelter, rest and exercise. If you or your employee cannot satisfy these needs, functioning will be inefficient and management of them will be almost impossible.

Since we human beings are social animals, we need that interaction we require pleasant relations with other people (supervisors, peers, etc.), a sense of belonging or being needed, and a desire for status.

If you have been in management for a long period, you have encountered people who would forgo a raise in salary in order to achieve a title that had status associated with it. Strange as it may see, as we shall see in later chapters, money is not the most significant motivator.

In addition, if that pleasant social interaction is not present, the employees tend to sulk and decrease normal communication. This creates the cycle of lower production and no communication; then less communication so the production drops. Therefore this interaction is mandatory if a department is to function well.

As an aside, this does not mean that everyone must like each other for success to follow. It does mean that people can agree to disagree and then go on about the business of the company.

Therefore such simple things as friendly greetings and conversation, team spirit, job titles, words of commendation for a job well done, etc. are your tools, if used with honesty and sincerity, to help meet the needs of your employees in social interaction.

All humans start life by being completely dependent on someone else for their very survival. As they grow, they become less dependent. A mature person needs to maintain a feeling of independence as well as the right to exercise some initiative.

A sense of personal achievement, realized through work, is a deep need. Few people can do their best unless that need is satisfied. Most people also want an opportunity for growth, to do something requiring more skills or versatility after they have mastered simpler tasks.

This challenge for your management skill is a priority because it involves the necessity to train and develop the employee, to delegate authority, to recognize skills and achievements and to offer the opportunity to progress to a more challenging position when ready.

As challenging as this sounds, most manufacturing operations do not overtly allow this kind of flexibility. A job is designed with a process and procedure, perhaps with a standard to be met, and the employee is expected to meet that standard by using the established process. Allowing flexibility in this environment is difficult. If you accept this as fact, your employees will never make progress and you will not satisfy their need for self expression.

Through the use of quality circles, team problem solving, group examination of processes and procedures to add value to the product, etc. etc., you can help your employees to achieve that satisfaction through participation. The process may be limiting but the analysis and initiative to reach for greater productivity, continuous improvement, and employee development is limited only by your desire for this type of motivation to satisfy your employees needs.

These human needs that need to be satisfied may seem overwhelming as you say" how can I do it?." As a manager your needs also need satisfying. This can be accomplished through use of your initiative, etc. to help your employees succeed.

You must gauge the individual's need and attempt to identify those that are most important to that individual. This knowledge enables you to determine what is necessary to motivate that person and , eventually, all of the those in your department, while ,at the same time, satisfying you and their most pressing needs. The combination of a well-motivated employee, who is satisfying his needs through his work experience, will result in an employee who is reaching his potential of efficient productivity. That is the goal of management!

WOW! I THINK I CAN REALLY LEAD! BUT, WHAT'S MY JOB REALLY?

You can read a hundred books and get two hundred definitions of management. most are couched in academia, are long, complicated, and make no sense at all. So what is it?

You can summarize management as:

"getting the job done through people."

Is it that simple? How is that possible?

A manager is responsible for more work that can be accomplished by one person, no matter how knowledgeable or efficient. Therefore it is necessary to coordinate the work of others to complete this assignment. Success as a manager is measured by the ability to do this.

Many years ago, a research team at the University of Michigan conducted several studies to determine the type of leadership that results in the highest productivity, lowest level of absence, lowest rate of turnover, and the greatest job satisfaction. The result of these studies was the identification of two different patterns of management, "production-centered: and "employee- centered."

The production-centered manager feels that the turning out of work is more important than anything else, and will jump in and do a lot of the work to reach that goal. In the process, little attention is paid to the people doing the work or the methods used. At times, threats and punishment are used to produce results. Volume production, regardless of method, is the "god."

The employee-centered manager expends effort to build a team that will cooperate and work well together. This manager is friendly, backs his people and trains them for their present and future jobs. Sight is never lost on the fact that attaining production levels are the goals of his responsibility and that of his department.

The result of the study seemed to show that the employee-centered manager had high production and high morale.

Remember that production-centered manager can be successful if the department is composed of employees who like that method of supervision. However, it is more difficult because you must endure the turnover and training in order to find that certain employee who can deal with that type of management personality.

A militaristic management style, while useful in some cases, does not allow for employees to fulfill the goals established by management. General goals give the employee some leeway as to how to reach that goal and this initiative produces growth and development in the employee.

I feel that the manager must be *humanistic* in that the employees prefer a manager who is likeable and reasonable. They feel freer to go to the manager about their job and personal problems.

A litany of attributes for a good manager, as far as employees are concerned, would be:
1. The manager is fair in dealing with people.
2. The manager has integrity and can be trusted to do what he says.
3. The manager has self control.

4. The manager understand the workers and lets them know what is expected of them in their jobs.
5. The manager maintains good discipline (positive intervention to be discussed later).
6. The manager gives credit for good work and does not absorb credit for other peoples work.
7. The manager inspires workers to turn out good work through good planning, quality expectations, and interpersonal relationships.
8. The manager knows his/her personal responsibilities as well as the rules and regulations of the company and can explain them clearly.
9. The manager is friendly and does not show any partiality.

These attributes and others form the foundation for leadership as well as successful management for your company through the prudent and efficient use of your employees.

Perhaps now, after reading this chapter, you can answer the question posed at the start of this section: If I were my employee, would I follow me?

I KNOW I CAN LEAD BUT WILL THEY FOLLOW?

This is probably one of the most difficult questions for any manager to answer. The true answer rests with the manager and how the employees are managed. Remember in the last chapter, we discussed you and your needs. Well, why should it come as a surprise to you that your employees have needs that must be satisfied for them to reach their full potential? Why would they be different in what they need our of their manager than what you need out of yours? Am I to try to remember what each individual employee wants and what makes each one "tick." The answer is a resounding "YES" if you want consistent, efficient production from each employee. That makes the question mark in the cartoon even bigger. How can I possibly do that?

This chapter will deal with methods of getting the best out of your people. In order to start this subject, you have to understand why people work in the first place.

The answer is obvious, isn't it? We work to make money.

This is true to some extent. But, in studies which we will discuss later, money was not the first motivating factor for either salaried or hourly employee nor was it the second. Understanding this phenomenon is the key to your success in discovering how to get people to follow your lead.

How often have we seen on TV or in the media a story about a person winning a large sum of money. The first question asked is "are you quitting your job?." If the amount is not in the millions, the person usually says "no." When questioned further, the person usually has some other reason for wanting to continue to work. In addition, some people with great needs and expenses might work long hours when welfare would pay more. Why? Because the money is not the motivating factor for that person. Pride, self-esteem, the feeling of accomplishment, etc. might be the motivator.

Strange as this sounds, most of your employees have different reasons for what they do and for what they will do for you. It is up to you to discover and use those reasons for success, yours and theirs.

Many theories have been developed on the subject of motivation by psychologists, sociologists, economists, industrialists and other "ists" as well as combination of these "ists." They have studied groups of workers ranging from office workers at the Prudential Insurance Company to internal organ sorters and washers at a hog slaughterhouse in London. Conclusions have been drawn from projects as different as studying six women sitting on a long bench assembling telephone relays at the highest rate ever recorded at the time (despite the addition of or withdrawal of rest periods, shorter hours, increased pay, adequate lighting, or other benefits), to watching and recording the behavior of chimpanzees that had been trained to perform simple motor tasks in return for poker chips which they could exchange for food and water (and they stopped working after they had accumulated 20 or 30 chips). Based upon the above, you can see why the literature on motivation is so fascinating. However, you can also see the conclusions do not result in a clear cut program for motivation of your employees.

It is probably better for us to explore certain principles that adapt to the office or plant environment. Remember that these are not rules but guidelines to help you to determine how to motivate each individual that you manage.

Motivation has been described as bringing out the best that a person has to offer within their own capabilities. In other words, the employee is capable and motivation inspires them to reach their full capabilities in their job.

Before you can motivate, you must understand the basic tenet of why people work.

YOU MEAN I DON'T HAVE TO THROW MONEY AT PEOPLE TO MAKE THEM WORK?

The manager has many raw materials with which to mold a quality product. However, the most complicated is a person because it must be recognized that every individual is different from all the others. *To motivate people it is necessary to get to know them and identify their individual needs and desires.*

As mentioned in the last chapter, Maslow had his "need hierarchy" of needs and that people worked to satisfy these needs. The hierarchy exists because you must satisfy the basic needs (hunger, thirst, security, health, etc.) before you can build and satisfy the higher needs (those of belonging, esteem, and self-actualization). Self actualization is a fancy term but all it means is reaching your greatest potential for self fulfillment and personal growth. Therefore Maslow would say that the effective manager must be sensitive to the needs of the individual in order to try to understand what that individual is trying to achieve by working and what the manager must do to draw the maximum performance out of that individual.

Let's say that there is an opening in your department at the highest salary grade and you have five people who wish to bid on the position and who are qualified. Were you to see the motivator for each of the employees, you might see the following:

> Tom wants the job because all his buddies are at that salary grade and he wants to be on a par with his friends.
>
> Mary wants the job because, as a single mother, she wants to buy a house and this position would help her to do that.
>
> John wants the job because it would make him more senior within the department and that would protect him in case of a layoff.

Amelia feels that she has not been recognized for her potential and performance in the past. This job would fulfill her expectations.

Paul feels that he is the best qualified and has put in his time within the organization. On the basis of seniority alone, he should get the job.

Your job is now even more interesting. Why? Because you only have one job available and will give it to one of the above allowing that person to achieve. BUT what of the other four?

If you do not know the individual motivator in each case, you cannot know the depths to which each one will sink when they do not succeed. Remember, to that person, their reason in the most important reason for them. Therefore you have rejected them and their reason for success. Sounds like fun, n'est pas?

Has this riddle been created just to frustrate you? No, this happens all the time and it does not matter in what company you toil, this is the real world. This is the type of motivational problem that you can face each day.

The bottom line in this equation is that, by knowing the individual's motivational factor, you can work with that individual to give them more security, more overtime to get more money, more status, or more training for that individual to succeed. And you MUST do this in order to keep these employees working toward your company's goals.

This example points up the variety of needs that can exist in people, often kept concealed, or worse for the manager, explained in other terms as well as the importance of the manager determining the true needs of the individual and responding to them.

It seems obvious that people work for a variety of reasons, based on their individual needs. It also seems obvious that money is only one reason, often far from the most important, and that you MUST know your employees well to determine their true motives for performing as they do (good or bad), and what you can do to lead them to use their abilities to perform even more efficiently.

SO YOU CAN'T LEAD IF NEEDS BEYOND MY CONTROL ARE MISSING?

Essentially this is true. The basic needs or rewards exist outside the work activity itself and tend to be beyond your immediate control. Such factors as fair wages, fringe benefits, vacations with pay, etc. must exist for a person to want to come to work. They do not motivate a person toward efficient work. They just allow them to show up for work.

Motivators are factors that have an uplifting effect on performance and attitude. They are intrinsic in the work itself. In fact the satisfaction or self actualization to the employee usually occurs during the activity of the work itself.

It is the corporate responsibility to meet the basic needs so that it can recruit workers for you to motivate. On its part, it must be competitive in the labor market in order to draw potentially good employees. If the corporation does not tend to these labor costs, then you will tend to have employees who have no motivation to improve. Why? Because, if they are good employees, they will be looking for other work where their basic needs are satisfied BEFORE they begin the actual job. If they are not necessarily good employees, they will tend to drift to look for something a little bit better. In either case, you lose because your turnover and training costs are extremely high and production efficiency suffers from lack of stability.

Motivators are largely non-financial satisfactions that arise out of the job itself. They will not operate without the basic needs being satisfied. But, if the basics are there, motivators are the tools that you can use to bring out the best in your employees.

Motivators consist in such things as freedom to exercise initiative and ingenuity; to experiment; to handle the problems of the job itself in a personal way; to earn deserved and honestly expressed praise; to know the purpose of the work; to know the results of the effort; to compete without being criticized or losing status in the process; to experience personal progress in ability; to realize a sense of achievement; to participate as a member of a group; to take part in group decisions about the work; to know that the work is important; to avoid boredom on the job, etc.

If the above are truly motivators, and they are, and your employees are individuals, and they are, then each motivator does not apply equally or at all to each individual. You get the best from your employee by knowing which one produces the best result for you and the person.

By *KNOWING YOUR EMPLOYEES*, you can see the relationship that each wants from the job and you can use that knowledge to satisfy both needs.

HOW DO I KNOW WHAT'S *REALLY* IMPORTANT TO AN INDIVIDUAL?

Hard work with that employee is the only answer to that question. However, as a guide, studies have been done with hourly and salaried personnel over the years. Let's look at the study for each and try to determine when the study was completed. These studies were reported in *Psychology* in Industry by Norman R.F. Maier and published by Houghton Mifflin.

This first study evaluated a composite group consisting of women factory workers, department store workers, miscellaneous production workers, union workers and non-union workers. All toll the study consisted of about 25,000 hourly people. The work factors that motivated this group are as follows:

WORK FACTOR	**RANK**
Steady work	1
Opportunity for advancement	2
High pay	3
Opportunity to learn a job	4
Comfortable working conditions	5
Good boss	6

Good working companions	7
Opportunity to use own ideas	8
Good hours	9
Easy work	10

Notice carefully that the chief motivator was not money but security. This is something that is very hard to predict in the '90s and will be even harder to provide in the next century IF the corporation is not able to be very flexible and the workers accept change as a way of life.

Look at the second motivator to the hourly work force. Many of us have felt in the past that we, as managers, did not need to worry about that factor since the "cream would rise to the top" and we could promote accordingly. However, if this is such a big motivator for people in general, that means we have to provide development opportunities for our employees so that they can advance when the time comes. How many of our employees are not motivated in their work because we do not provide that development or write it off as unimportant?

I was very surprised that having a good boss was more important to hourly workers than having good peers, good hours and easy work. This places the emphasis on the manner we deal with our employees as a chief motivator in their success as well as in your success.

This survey was conducted in *1965*. Can you believe that? Security was a chief issue in a time of economic stability and growth. Note that this has not changed today. It is even more important because of the "downsizing', "rightsizing," etc. of corporations and the economic insecurity that has pervaded the '80s and '90s. This will not change in the next century. This also makes the continuous improvement projects of quality control even more important to the survival and security of the hourly work force.

Is there a difference between hourly workers and managers? Yes, to some degree the satisfaction of needs in the management group is more sophisticated in what they want out of work. The survey dealing with management produced the following factors:

WORK FACTOR	RANK
Achievement	1
Recognition	2
Work itself	3
Responsibility	4
Advancement	5
Salary	6
Possibility of growth	7
Interpersonal Relationships	8
Status	9
Working conditions	10
Job security	11

Now that is a shocker! Job security has gone from number 1 with the hourly group to last in the management group. Why? The basic answer is that if all of the preceding factors are being met, the value of the manager is very high to the corporation and the job security takes care of itself, in most cases. In other words, if you do your job well, you don't worry about security. It is there!

When making comparisons between hourly and management, the obvious needs to be satisfied vary widely. The hourly need more basic satisfiers, the management group more sophisticated. However, both groups want to advance, to use their own ingenuity to advance, to achieve in a clean, well run company, and to feel the need to be wanted and valuable to that company.

This second survey was included in *The Motivation to Work* by Frederick Herzberg, John Wiley and Sons. This study was done in *1959*.

These studies have been used because the work factors that are motivators have not changed in all of these years. Some may have changed position relative to the others but they do give you the hard motivators that really get people to do the job that you ask.

IF I CAN LEAD, HOW CAN I GET THEM TO FOLLOW?

It has been pointed out many times in this work already that individuals vary in their needs and that motivational; approaches must be tailored to the individual. Some needs are quite constant throughout a person's life, whereas others may vary from day to day.

A person who needs praise will probably seek it through life but that same person may need to be reassured about his/her value to the department and company only occasionally. In this case, the praise that is needed pertains to projects that are personally performed rather than the overall worth of that individual.

Individuals differ as to the work units, departments and manager who are in charge of them. Therefore one set of rules or suggestions would not be appropriate as applying to every situation. Thus the following suggestions are for your evaluation and use in the specific situations that you find and they may or may not work, depending upon your knowledge of the individual and that person's needs.

You might attempt to use more "democratic" rather than "authoritarian" methods of management. Can certain of your employees function effectively with very little direct supervisory control? Will they improve their performance if you allow them to participate in goal setting, decision making and determining methods of doing their jobs?

Encourage suggestions from everyone in your group. Do not be judgmental on the suggestions, give them respect. Keep an open mind and listen to what the employee is saying and use their suggestions if possible. Involve your employees in the work of the department through meetings with the group and keep them informed of their part in the overall progress of the department and company. Encourage them to think of their daily work as a career not just a job.

Tailor praise and criticism to your understanding of the needs of that individual. Treat all with understanding, courtesy and consideration; be firm and fair. This suggestion does not mean that you cannot express emotion, even anger, at performance. However, the method that you use could be critical. For example, you are meeting with an employee who has made a serious error on the job. Instead of hollering and berating the employee (NOTE: it does not hurt for you to look at yourself in this area and see if you lose your temper easily, etc.), advise the employee at the start in this manner: "John, this error has caused this department time and money and I am very upset and angry about it! Now, let's examine how it happened and what we can do to prevent it from happening again.." This scenario advises the employee that an error has been made that is serious. It also advises him that you are angry BUT under control. Finally, it allows for progression to make the situation better and correct future problems. Loss of control puts the employee in a defensive posture and you will not succeed in teaching that employee *how to improve*.

Another suggestion is to remember that nervousness and uneasiness are contagious. If you show these to your employees, they will become nervous without knowing why or if they should be nervous. It is your job to display competence, confidence and a positive well motivated appearance to your employees so they can imitate you. It is recognized that this is very hard when problems are serious and, at times, overwhelming.

BUT this is a motivator. *Use it or lose it!*

Another suggestion that you may use is to set the groundwork in your department for any changes that you are going to make. Try not to surprise anyone. In the environment of chaos, change is constant but you still must or should explain and "sell" changes so they will accept them and adapt to them readily.

Take advantage of the leadership within the group. The "informal leaders" that always seem to exist in a unit can be a key to getting your message across to the other employees. Secure the cooperation and agreement of these persons on goals, methods, etc. and they will help you get the work done through the other people.

These suggestions are just starting points for your efforts in improving your methods of motivating your employees. The important point to remember here is that you *MUST* do something in the area of motivation to be a fully effective leader.

WILL I EVER UNDERSTAND PEOPLE?

The enormity of this question leads to a "no" answer. However, each day that you move forward and learn a new motivational tool for that individual means that you are gaining understanding. This process is ongoing and will never end because life is dynamic and chaotic. Remember if you had this question pegged, life would be a bore. Now it is a constant challenge.

If your major operating cost is your payroll, it follows that your main job as a manager is to realize your employees full potential. So you must learn or begin to learn how to handle people. Look at your own experiences with your managers and see how one handled you and how another handled you. Was there a difference? Did either care about you? Did either inspire you to be better? If so, model yourself after that one and ignore the one who was not people oriented. Herein lies another secret to success.

HINTS ABOUT SUCCESSFUL MOTIVATION

RECOGNIZE THE INDIVIDUAL—To the employee, individual recognition is the most important condition of work. All of us have pride. We want to feel important. We have to belong to something because we are social animals. We must be valuable to someone. Our efforts must be noticed and acknowledged.

Your job is to demonstrate a genuine personal interest in each of your employees. That interest will be returned with dividends through increased enthusiasm toward the job, the department, the company and, most important, towards you.

KEEP AN OPEN DOOR—How many times have we heard " my door is always open " as we hear the sound of the door slamming behind that manager? This item means that you should always be willing to listen. Listening, as we shall see later in this book, is the key to determining what is really important to the person and what needs to be done to correct problems. It's easier to solve problems when you know what they are instead of spinning your wheels in sand.

KEEP EMPLOYEES INFORMED—Most employees cannot see the department and company goals because they are not part of that communication process. You are! Pass on the information, if you can, to the employees. Let them know how their job contributes to the overall success of the product and the company. People can only show initiative when they know what is expected of them and the department. This is not privileged information; it is information needed for success and motivation as well as for keeping the interest of your employees high enough to achieve that success.

REWARD GOOD WORK—Many managers only let a person know how they are performing during review time. A review should never be a surprise to an employee because you have spoken to them daily about their successes and failures and helped them to correct the bad and continue the good. We all have a certain feeling of insecurity, no matter what our position. That ability to let us know how we are doing allows us to improve and stay motivated throughout the year. Just make sure that this information is constructive and sincere. Your employee will know. Don't you?

BE FIRM—Employees consider this the first quality of leadership. Employees do not want a wimp for a boss. They have enough trouble in their lives and jobs without have to try to manage too because you won't make a decision. Firmness is not a disadvantage. You will not be respected without it. You have rules and regulations and your employees expect you to enforce them for their benefit as well as for the company's.

BE FAIR—You probably like some employees more than others. This is normal. However, you cannot let this enter into your dealing with them. Treat your employees impartially and assign work in the same way. Recognize only job merit.

BE FRANK—People want to know how they are doing. They can best improve when they have a frank appraisal of their strong and weak points. Most employees will appreciate your interest in them and their progress, if you do it well and he honest.

BE UNSELFISH—There has never been a monopoly on good ideas. Seek them from your employees and give them credit for them. When the department does well, share the credit with all of the employees. This will aid in your motivation toward the next time because they know that all share in the praise.

These first chapters have tried to let you determine if you can lead and how to do that. It doesn't matter whether you manage 2,5,10,100,1000 or more, the principles in these chapters will stand you well now and into the next century. This is true because you will manage *people*. People's habits and clothes may change But, as the studies mentioned showed, the motivators and get people into action are the same and the needs and wants are the same. Therefore the principles are the same.

Treat each person as an individual about whom you care and success is yours.

WHY DO I HAVE SUCH TROUBLE GETTING THEM TO UNDERSTAND WHAT I WANT DONE?

"Here it comes! I just know that he's going to talk about *communication*. I have heard that word so often and have been preached to about it so much that it doesn't have much meaning anymore."

How true that statement is! We have heard it often in management and have tried to manage through effective communication from day one. However, it sometimes feels that communication is as slippery as the orange seed that has fallen to the floor and we are trying to pick it up. It's right in front of us but we can't set our hand on it for the moment. Even when we pick it up, it feels like it is going to slip away before we can throw it in the trash.

So when we try to understand and use effective communication, we need to understand the basics so that we don't wind up like our friend in the picture.

What comes next is not a revelation and should not be. It is a re-awakening of things that you already know but have pushed aside as old fashioned or too simple for our complex world of business. The twenty-first century, like all previous centuries will revolve around our understanding of how to get a message across to other people. It's not so hard if we understand the basics. Let's look at some of them!

VOICES, VOICES, VOICES, I HEAR THEM, BUT WHAT ARE THEY SAYING?

"When I am giving someone instructions, I know that I am clear, concise and to the point. But I don't understand why that person may or may not do what I have asked. This makes me angry and I have to rush to correct a situation that never should have happened in the first place. Why? Why? Why?"

Perhaps the main answer to this often asked question is that the person did not hear clearly what you were saying. Since you were, you felt, so clear, how could this happen?

Mainly, any form of communication requires a sender and receiver. Communication, then, is the process through which messages are sent and received. This is a very "active" process which is in constant change caused by a wide variety of elements within the sender, receiver, environment, cultural backgrounds, light, temperature, physical condition of each and on and on. In some cases, it is a wonder that a message comes through and is understood at all.

Let's look at this process in the form of a baseball pitcher and catcher. When the pitcher throws a straight fastball, it travels through a medium (air) and hits the catcher's glove by the most direct means. There is very little interference from the air and the ball can be seen to be straight, hard and fast. However, if the pitcher throws a curve, slider or knuckleball, the rotation and other elements make the ball act strangely and the catcher could be fooled if he did not know what the pitcher was throwing. In other words, the ball would not go where the catcher expected and he did not receive the message of the change.

In the same way, communication requires a sender to throw the message straight and hard so that it penetrates its medium (whatever) and hits the receiver clearly. Thus, the message is understood. Then the receiver send a message back to the sender indicating whether the message was clear or not. It is critical in management, as in life, that the sender understand that the message was understood as meant.

The critical nature of this simple statement is magnified because of the increased complexity of modern technology in manufacturing, service, and other industries. Without understanding, the product will not be properly made, the turnover rate will increase, and the profit may not be made.

A good manager is one whose verbal and non-verbal messages are consistent. That is shown in employees who might look at their manager as one who says one thing and means another.

In this case the non-verbal messages are offsetting the verbal messages and the employees are confused about what is really going on in the workplace. The object of the baseball game is to confuse the batter, not the catcher. At work, no one should be confused as to what needs to be done, how is should be done and by whom.

A manager who is an effective leader accomplishes the Company's goals because the employees want to do their jobs rather than because they have to do them. They want to because they know what is expected and they have all the help they need to get the job done. This inspires and motivates the employee toward continuous improvement and a quality product.

Let's consider what keeps the message from being understood.

Between the sender and the receiver, there is a filtering screen. This screen can be very porous and messages are received, as meant, almost all of the time or the screen can be very dense and messages are hardly received at all. What makes this screen porous or dense?

Initially we could say that as long as both parties speak the same language, messages are easily sent and received. However, as you already know, this is not the easy answer. Even speaking the same language (i.e. English) does not promote understanding automatically because different regions of the country have dialects, idioms, and phrases that have somewhat unusual meanings in other regions of the country.

Let's compound this regional dialect problem by the speed with which we speak, faster in the North, slower in the South, deliberate in New England, and with a language in California that defies a single adjective.

If we add to this list the educational levels of sender and receiver, motivational levels of both parties, the temperature of the environment, the cultural differences, the ethnic backgrounds, the outside noise levels, etc., it is a wonder that anything comes across clearly.

This is the very reason why we must concentrate so hard on effective communication.

NOW THAT THE PROBLEM IS CLEAR, HOW CAN WE COMMUNICATE CLEARLY?

In order to know how, we need to know or attempt to know what is the definition of communication. Certainly, you can look up a definition in the dictionary as easily as I can. Therefore I would like to paraphrase a definition that has some elements that we can examine.

"Communication involves

(a) a sharing of information (any type);

(b) between a sender and receiver;

(c) that results in;

(d) an understanding of both parties."

SHARING OF INFORMATION—This is a critical part of the definition because a sharing is required for effective communication. The receiver must be a participant in the process. If the receiver, for whatever reason, does not want to share the information, THERE IS NO COMMUNICATION. This information to be shared can be verbal or non-verbal. It is up to you to create the environment as well as understand the receiver well enough to know how best to share your information.

We are back to understanding your individual employees and they are different. What works for one in communication might not work for anyone else in your department. Yet, you have to get the same message across to all employees in the department. Therefore your knowledge of each employee helps you to create the environment for sharing and you have a better chance of success with that individual.

A political example comes to mind. If a conservative Republican is speaking to a liberal Democrat, the chances for communication are lessened unless both parties are willing to participate with an open mind. The odds are low in this case. The same is true if you are trying to get an employee to understand something new when all of his background is cemented in another environment. Therefore the sharing of information must be in an environment that gives the message a chance of success in reaching the receiver.

BETWEEN A SENDER AND RECEIVER—In effect we do need two to communicate. Two people are not necessarily required. A memo, poster, body language, etc. can be a player with you as the receiver. However, communication cannot exist if you are talking to yourself. You can reason but you can't communicate.

THAT RESULTS IN—Unless there are results from the sending and receiving, there is no communication. If the results are not what were desired from the message, clearly there was no sharing of information between the sender and receiver.

AN UNDERSTANDING OF BOTH PARTIES—This critical part demonstrates that what was heard was what you said.

You, as the manager, must be proficient in communicating because nothing happens within the Company unless the action has been preceded by communication of some sort. Therefore the group and your effectiveness largely depends upon your ability to communicate, both sending and receiving, with your employees.

WHAT FORM DOES COMMUNICATION TAKE?

Within a Company, you can have communications that are official or formal as well as unofficial and unplanned types.

The official communications can be of several types. Among them are:

1. Written (memos, letters, policies and procedures, manuals, bulletin boards, pictures, graphs, charts, films, etc. These are primarily aimed at the receiver's eyes. They tend to be so rigid that they do not permit questioning by the receiver and require understanding

directly from the written word. For those of us who have written memos, policies, etc. this form is fraught with danger in that the receiver may not see things the way we do and not get the correct message. We, in turn, get angry because we have to re-write the document in order to get the receiver to understand.

2. Spoken communications directed at the receiver's ears. (telephone messages, radios, recordings, intercoms, paging, etc.) These can be precise or casual and discussions and/or questions are possible.

3. A combination of written and oral is the most effective because it involves two senses and permits an exchange of ideas, questions and assurances on the part of both parties of understanding.

4. Actions are powerful forces of communications. Your actions indicate to your department the type of person you are as well as how you deal with situations. Actions can be used effectively to emphasize your spoken communications but they must be sincere and used with care.

5. Body language is a most effective method of communication because it tends to allow others to see how you really feel about a situation not what you are saying about that issue. For example, if you are listening to an employee with your arms crossed, you are visually setting up a barrier, between you and the employee, allowing the employee to feel that you do not want to hear what is being said or that you do not believe what is being said. This language betrays your words and leaves you open to the perception of a lie even when you allegedly agree with what is being said.

All of these official techniques of communication must be coupled with your understanding of each employee in your department so that you can use the most effective method at any given time to assure that your message is being received as meant.

Not an easy task, is it?

Unofficial forms of communication, while not the best in terms of accuracy, consist of rumors and the age old "grapevine" as examples. Frankly, we would all like to ignore these forms because they tend to be wrong and they cause a lot of anguish or, worse still, they are often right on information that is confidential and you have trouble explaining why this information is not public or you have to less than honest in your responses to some sensitive information.

However, the important thing for you to remember in this category is that you must pay attention to this form and, perhaps, even use it to your advantage on occasion,

When you encounter rumors that are inaccurate or partially accurate, you must know that they are circulating on the floor and that people are believing them because management is not giving them any other alternative to the rumor. In these situations, you can take the time to explain what you can and point out the inaccuracies and put your employee's minds to rest. If you don't have an answer to the rumor, find out if there is an answer that you can share. Make sure that you share only accurate information with your employees for the same reasons mentioned in all of the foregoing pages.

Wait a minute? Didn't you just say that we might have to share information that is less than honest? Perhaps you may at the request of the corporation. It is then up to you and your code of ethics as to whether you do this. Remember you do have a choice as long as you understand the risks in making that choice.

To correct rumors and the grapevine, you should provide accurate information so the employees understand that your word is to be believed. Your employees will respect you if you tell them that you are knowledgeable on the issue but need more information before you can share it with them. This will give you more time and let the employees know that you are getting the "straight scope" for them. The rumor will subside until you get the answer.

The most embarrassing rumor/grapevine is when you leave a meeting where you have discussed a sensitive subject, go out on the floor, and the employees already know about it and are discussing it themselves. Radar? ESP? Spies? Who knows? But the information is usually accurate and you have just heard about it.

If for no other reason, you must pay attention to this form of communication.

Your use of the grapevine is necessary sometimes to spread information (accurate) without the use of formal statements, policies, etc. In these situations, you control the information and the amount that is being shared with the staff and your department. Perhaps, this is the only area of informal communication where you have some control. Remember that the information needs to be spread so it is received as meant not as interpreted by various levels. Therefore caution must be urged in the use of this method of communication.

ATTENTION, EMPLOYEES! DO THIS! DO THAT!

Somewhat military, isn't it? But, truly, we survive and manage through the issuance of orders and instructions. You have the authority to use these tools to direct people to get the work done. Your employees understand and accept this authority because it is a part of our lives. They have come to work believing that the supervisor and manager has a right to request certain actions from them and they have a duty to act as directed. If they choose not to follow the instructions, then they have chosen to leave or remove themselves from the environment wherein the instructions were issued. Simply, no?

However, you, too, have a responsibility to recognize that your issuance of orders and instructions affects your employees' needs for security and recognition through the manner in which you give them. The efficiency of your department and your employees depends on your proficiency in communicating what you want done and how.

Instructions need to be given clearly and concisely so your people will know what is desire of them. However, there are certain steps that will help you to accomplish the clarity of your message.

Before discussing these steps, let me point out that they are not something new and exciting. We have all heard them so many times that it is very difficult to attribute an author for an accurate footnote. If researched, they would probably go back to the cave dwellers so they could get their meat and plan their journeys. Therefore do not expect revelations. But remember that these steps have stood the test of time and they work now and will into the twenty first century and beyond.

SUPER STEPS:

1. PLANNING—When you have received your work instructions and assignment, make a plan for the accomplishment of that task. Determine what information the employees must have in order to accomplish this task and how you will have to explain it to them. What equipment or tools will be necessary, etc.

This process is THE foundation to the success of your work. Poor planning leads to poor production.

2. PREPARING—If you were a lawyer, doctor, engineer, machinist, janitor, or domestic engineer, there is no substitute for preparation, preparation, preparation. This means that you will have assembled all of the facts, etc. and equip yourself to issue the necessary orders and instructions clearly and concisely as well as be in a position to discuss your instructions intelligently.

3. PRESENTING—remember that people are different. Therefore the issuance of your instructions must be tailored to the individual for them to be most effective. You might accomplish this by describing the entire project to the department and then getting with the individuals to advise them how they are expected to participate in the accomplishment of the project goals. In this way, you advise all and give the individual the attention needed for the task.

Why spend the time? Because you are sure that each employee understands the purpose of HIS or HER work and how it fits into the overall goals of the department. If one employee is confused, that affects the quality of the team. Phrasing your order or instruction in the form of a request or suggestion might make the employee part of the solution rather than one who could create more problems. An order will be obeyed but will it be obeyed with the enthusiasm generated by the employees' cooperation rather than employees' requirement to follow instructions or lose the job?

In effect, how you issue the instruction will lead to success or failure because it must be issued to each individual so they hear the message as meant.

4. VERIFYING—It is imperative that you find out if the employee understands your instructions. This "feedback" allows you to make changes in the instructions, discover errors in your planning or preparation as well as help your employee to improve and be successful.

Your get feedback by asking questions, etc. If your instructions are lengthy and complex and the employee does not ask questions, something is wrong. Find out what is wrong and correct it. Even brilliant employees have trouble with complex instructions. Make sure they understand.

This is also the time to ask the employee for suggestions on how the work can be done better, faster, or with value added to the quality of the product. Make the employee past of the solution. (Sound familiar?) This is not only a motivational technique but utilizes all of the employees' creative juices to get the best product at the lowest cost. If that employee's idea is acceptable and you use it, that employee will make sure that it works as well as be motivated to provide you with more suggestions in the future.

5. ACTION—This step can only be accomplished by the employee. It is the actual carrying out of the instructions. If you have done well, the end result will be what you want. If the communication was not clear, etc., the result will be obvious.

It is important to note here that you must give the employee a chance to succeed and let the job be done without distraction. If you picked the right employees and you lead and motivated well and communicated clearly, you will get the quality product.

6. FOLLOW UP—It is always wise to follow up with the employee while the job is being done to see how he is coming and whether there are any snags that you can help him overcome or if there are any new ideas to increase the value of the end result. This step enables you to gauge progress and spot trouble before time is wasted or damage done.

7. APPRAISING—When the task is completed, you should review the entire process and objectively determine whether it was performed accurately, efficiently and economically as a result of your efforts and those of your employees.

This is also the time to discuss the project with your employees in order to determine how he felt about the task and what could be done to make the process easier the next time. The appraising step is a time to evaluate your employees' performance but it is also a time to measure your expectations against the final result.

As I said several pages ago, there are no revelations here. But there is a great deal of common sense THAT HAS WORKED over the centuries. Why ignore a good thing? Use it and improve on it as you see fit. But never ignore the success that these steps have given the efficient, modern manager.

There is an old Irish saying that goes "you have to know how to tell a person to go to h—and have him look forward to getting there."

In essence, that summaries the "C" word. You have to be able to tell people the good and the bad so that each individual understand your message. You have made the screen very porous so your true meaning comes through no matter what other factors affect that individual.

A challenge? Yes!Impossible? No! Look around you at all of the successful managers, leaders, parents, artists, musicians, etc. Why are they successful? Because they can get their message across as meant.

So can you, if you want to and will spend the time to do it right!

HOW DO MY EMPLOYEES RESEMBLE THE CHARACTERS ON THE RIGHT?
OR
WHEN I SAY "RIGHT," WHY DO THEY INVARIABLY GO "LEFT"?

It's time to spend some more time on communication, but not the type that involves speaking or writing. This time we need to spend some time on the Art of Listening.

This chapter is not long but it is one of the most important ideas in this book. Why? Because it makes no difference how good we are in conveying our message, if we are not understood.

The basics for understanding rest not totally with your ability to send a message. A great deal depends on the receiver's ability to concentrate and receive your message as it is meant. For the doubters, this is a learned skill akin to an art in itself. Let's see what this means!

For the moment, let's look at our own ability to listen. Have you, in the past, misunderstood some direction; not followed a verbal order; thought you understood what was required only to find out that you were wrong; thought you were listening carefully and missed a lot of information? If these things have not happened to you, you already have developed this Art and should skip to the next chapter. For most of you, you can now see the problems that your employees can have. They are not trying to ignore you and your directions. They just have not listened well enough.

Now that you see that this has happened to you in the past. Let's see if we can identify some of the causes and/or solutions to the problem as well as develop listening into an art .

In the last chapter, we spoke about a screen between the sender and receiver. The density of that screen determines if the message is received as sent. (During this entire topic, I am assuming that the receiver is not intentionally receiving messages poorly.)

There are two types of obstacles that get in the way of getting accurate information. These are concrete obstacles and psychological obstacles. Both are severe "screens" to accurate information if you do not recognize them and overcome their power. Yes, "POWER" is the correct word here because these obstacles can prohibit information from being conveyed.

The concrete obstacles have been stated many times and there is no need to re-invent them in a new context. Included in this group are:

- **LIGHTING**—if the room is too light or too dark or there is a glare on the paper, screen, or on your shiny forehead, there is a distraction.
- **NOISE**—too much noise distracts automatically. However, we humans have a capacity to block out sounds. In the case of noise, if there is too much we consciously block it. If you are consciously blocking something, is it not reasonable that you could block the message out along with the noise or, at the very least, not hear the whole message. You are trying so hard to keep sound out that you keep out more than you want and then don't hear what you are supposed to hear.
- **TEMPERATURE**—too hot or too cold makes your body react to the temperature not to the message. It's easier for the sender in this case than the receiver because the receiver has to concentrate on acquiring new information while the sender knows what is being said or written.
- **FATIGUE OR ILLNESS**—either of these situations need no analysis because it is hard to concentrate when you don't feel up to par.
- **HEARING LOSS**—this physical anomaly is very real for all employees, especially as we age. In addition, it is a condition that we do not admit to openly. Perhaps

we stay in constant denial in this regard and miss much information that cannot be retrieved because we do not admit the problem and seek corrective action.

The psychological obstacles to listening include:

- **INDIFFERENCE**—I just don't care what you are saying or no matter what you say, I will not change my mind. As a manager, if you are indifferent, you show boredom in your position or a contempt toward the job, your employees, or both. Overcoming this monster in management requires a great deal of self motivation, enthusiasm, and education to enrich the position so that it is exciting. Failure to overcome this element should result in leaving your position, voluntarily or involuntarily.
- **PREOCCUPATION**—In order to succeed in listening, you must devote your entire effort and attention to the process. If you cannot do this, postpone any session or meeting until you can concentrate fully on what is being said.
- **PREJUDICE**—If your opinion is strong about a certain issue or person, your ability to accept, through listening, another point of view is almost nil. In effect, you are approaching the situation with a closed mind. This happens many times in grievance proceedings or union negotiations. The opposition always seems to have a strong opinion without wanting to listen to any of the facts in the case. Therefore the facts do not spoil the pre-set opinion.
- **OVERLY SENSITIVE**—A person who is too sensitive to comments cannot listen to something negative, personal affronts, threats, etc. and not react to them. The successful manager is able to listen calmly and objectively and discuss the issues. Again it is fruitless to argue a valid point ,when no one is listening ,because no one wins ever. If you listen negatively

because you are too sensitive, no positive result will come out of your effort.

IT'S SO HARD TO LISTEN ACTIVELY, WHEN THE SENDER'S INFO IS NOT INTERESTING. HOW CAN YOU DO IT?

We have talked enough about the obstacles to listening. It is now time to determine an appropriate answer to the above question.

Listening is a *positive* act that requires *energy*. Whoa! Wait a minute! If I am just sitting or standing there passively trying to listen to what is being said, how can that require *energy*?

The energy comes from you wanting to understand what is being said. Therefore you must attempt to hear and interpret what the speaker is saying. Sure, some of the data is nonsense, some is not. But your mind must be so charged that you can determine what is and what is not. The energy comes from the sifting of information *that you have heard*. In addition, you have to interpret the motives, intentions and meanings of the sender so you get the correct message. How can you do this passively? NOT POSSIBLE!!!

Your outward appearance of calmness and being relaxed does not mirror your mind because you are actively trying to hear everything and understand it.

Physically, and sometimes mentally, people tend to assume a very relaxed posture when they listen. However, to exert that positive energy you should sit up and lean forward in your seat so that you reflect that your mind is alert and your systems charged in trying to understand what is being said. Consequently, if you do not understand what is being said, you can ask appropriate questions immediately instead of trying to remember the point later and then trying to determine why you did not understand it in the first place. Immediate activity clears up the mud before it clouds the water.

In the book *The Process of Management* by William Newman and Charles Summer, nine guidelines for listening have been outlined based on many years of experience in clinical psychology, psychiatry and non directed interviewing in industry. They are shown below because they tend to address the *active* nature of listening and give you some help in achieving that state.

- Listen patiently to what is being said even though you may believe it to be wrong or irrelevant. The importance of that statement relates to the respect that you are giving the other party as well as recognition of ideas other than your own. This process is hard especially when you want to correct or lead someone before you have heard them out. Harder still is the patience required when you have other pressing duties to perform and not enough time for this process.
- Try to understand the feeling the person is expressing as well as the intellectual content. Men and women express their feelings in different ways. In fact, the confusion of "feelings" has radically changed in the '80s and '90s especially along gender lines. Men had always been taught that they should not express their feelings. (Real men don't cry!, etc) Women, on the other hand were allowed to express themselves and their feelings openly. Today, this understanding of feelings has turned 180 degrees. Men are now told it is OK to be open about feelings and to express them. Women, especially in the business management areas, are told that they cannot express themselves as they had before. Therefore both sexes have somewhat confused gender roles with respect to their feelings, especially if they are over thirty-five years of age. Therefore this guideline becomes more difficult because we try to interpret feelings through our own eyes and not the eyes of the sender. What did he/she really mean?
- Restate the person's feeling briefly but accurately. In effect you are serving as a mirror to insure that you really understand the feeling expressed. Again, as it

being said, not later, state what you have heard and let the sender tell you if you have heard correctly.

- Allow time for the discussion to continue without interruption. Try not to make the conversation any more "authoritative" than it already is by virtue of your management position. Obviously, if you are issuing a discipline, the authoritative nature of the conversation is strong. If you are talking about an upcoming football game and you pick the winner, your status as a manager has nothing to do with the outcome of the ball game. Do not try to make it so! The person to whom you are speaking has as much right to his/her opinion as you do, no matter what their status in the company. Give them the time to express themselves and then move on.
- Avoid direct questions and arguments about facts. Avoid the "Prove it!" dialogue. Why? Because you may want the time to check the facts as you now know them against what is being said are the facts as the sender knows them. Then you do not have to make apologies because you did not have ALL the facts. But you only get that advantage IF you can avoid the confrontation and listen actively.
- When the other person does touch on a point that you want to know more about, simply repeat his statement as a question and let him respond again. This serves two purposes. One, it solicits more information from him. Two, it makes him rethink that position statement and add to or change it so that the intent is made clear. Either way, you get more clear information so you can understand what is being said.
- If the other person genuinely wants your viewpoint, be honest in your reply. In the listening stage, try to limit your viewpoints since they may repress what is trying to be said. However, *after* listening, your viewpoint

may be valuable to the sender. The difficult part is trying to figure out IF the sender really wants your viewpoint at all.
- Don't get emotionally involved yourself. Try to understand what is being said first, and defer your evaluation and reaction until later. As an example, in negotiating union contract, the opposition makes many statements that are not true or are misinterpreted or are inflammatory. If you react to them, as they are said, you have lost a competitive advantage because you have been placed in a defensive position. In most sports, it is hard to score points from the defensive side of the ball. Control is most important in your reaction to anything that you hear in your listening technique. Your reaction, verbally or through body language, reveals your thoughts, desires and emotions. Perhaps, you would like to keep your thoughts to yourself. By active listening, you give yourself that chance for control. Why give up an advantage?

Professors Newman and Summer have given us these guidelines to active listening. They make sense as well as given you a management advantage and, really, an advantage in life, in general, because not too many people think that listening takes energy. Don't waste that time or energy by not listening effectively.

In addition to giving us some ideas on how to listen, Newman and Summer also give us some concrete reasons for listening in the first place. Briefly, they are:
- Listening demonstrates your awareness of people. Remember that the central theme in this management primer is that you must concentrate on knowing the individual. How better to get to know that person than by listening to what he/she has to say?
- Listening promotes respect for you on the part of your employees. If you look at yourself and your relation-

ship with your boss or owner, do you feel more a part of the operation and connected to upper management if that person actually takes the time to listen to what you have to say? Why should your employees be any different in their relationship to you? Give them the attention they need and deserve and the rewards will come because they know that you care about them as individuals.

- Listening helps in handling grievances. How many times have you listened to or read about an employee grievance, concentrated on solving the perceived problem only to find out later that the real problem was not the one you thought it was? This comes from a lack of listening for content, feelings, implications and/or rule violations versus what is said in the original complaint. Don't get too upset over this comment! This happens more times than not, even to an experienced resolver of grievances. However we do need to use that active listening technique to try to eliminate what is not intended and to discover the core of the situation so that we can work on the real issue. This comes with time and *energy*.

- Listening improves efficiency. If communication flows freely, then understanding of the process is easier and efficiency is easier to achieve and maintain. Listening carefully helps you to identify problems early and solve them quickly. You also improve your employees' self esteem because you use their every day work experience to identify and solve those problems.

- Finally, listening helps you to evaluate your employees. Evaluate as in helping them to succeed not in judging their faults. (Certainly, you may have to do that with an uncooperative employee. However, education is far easier than termination as we will see in the training and discipline chapter of this book). A fair evaluation goes far beyond piece counts because you utilize your knowledge of that employee to assess how they can improve and be successful.

For most of us, we have heard many times about the "lack of communication" or the "communications breakdown" that has occurred. While the sender has to be clear in instructing or sending the message, the receiver must actively want to get the message correctly. Therefore the energy or charge from the sender must be received as energy or charge by the receiver for the message to be understood as sent. If there is no energy, some of that message might be lost and that might be critical to your success.

Be an **ACTIVE** listener who uses the proper **ENERGY** for your own **SUCCESS!**

**WAIT 'TILL HE GETS IN HERE!
I'LL WRING HIS NECK!
OR
HOW CAN HE BE SO
STUPID! I'VE TOLD HIM
OVER AND OVER AND OVER!**

Does this character resemble you when your employee makes mistake after mistake? How can you deal with this person? Will you "discipline" him like he's never been disciplined before? Will you fire him? Will you tell him how stupid he is? How much money he is costing the company? How much scrap he has created? How he could have hurt himself or others, or did? Darn, you're mad! I'm sure that you will tell him something!

There is no one, who is reading this book, who can say that they have not been in the above position before when something has gone wrong and you are responsible for what your employee has done. Responsible to your boss, not for the actual error.

In most cases, since managers have not always been trained well in dealing with people and problems, any or all of the above questions would be answered "yes." Will that correct the situation? Maybe, but probably not. Dealing with any type of discipline creates action and reaction in the boss and the employee. How you handle the discipline will dictate your success or failure as well as that of the disciplined employee.

Do you want the situation corrected, never to happen again with that employee? Do you want the employee to learn a lesson? Or do you just want to punish because you are mad and/or embarrassed that this has occurred?

This chapter will deal with discipline but in a positive way that is designed to elicit a positive result from the employee as well as establish a future employee who has really learned his lesson. How? Let's see!

The major change that we must make with regard to discipline is our understanding of what that really means. In Webster's New International Dictionary, the word "discipline" is defined as follows:
1. Teaching; instruction, tutoring.
2. That which is taught to pupils; teachings, learning, doctrine.
3. Training or course of training which corrects, molds, strengthens or perfects.
4. Punishment by one in authority.

Looking at that definition, what is the major difference between what we understand as discipline and what exists as the definition. (Recognize that a dictionary definition lists definitions in the order of priority).

If you are like most managers, you always believed that discipline was a form of punishment for doing something wrong. Yet, when you look at the definition, you see that "punishment" ranks fourth in priority of definition and "training and instruction" takes the first three places.

Sure! But we have rules to follow and people who violate those rules and they have to be "punished," don't they?

In fact, that is true. But why is that true?

Fortunately for most managers, people prefer to function as part of an organized, productive work unit rather than in an atmosphere where leadership is minimal, rules of behavior are disregarded and standards are so low that there is no challenge. Our employees prefer an environment where there is constructive discipline in evidence, and they respect the manager who maintains it. In such an environment, they can realize their greater satisfaction from their jobs and feel a sense of accomplishment. They are not inclined to object to reasonable requests or orders, nor to rules, regulations and procedures that are accepted as necessary for the productive performance of their jobs.

If that is so, then the definition must be wrong because we must "punish" those who violate the rules and regulations. Right? The answer to that question is "maybe yes and maybe no."

Using the full definition, the establishment of "good" discipline is your responsibility. You must, as an effective manager, introduce, explain, insure understanding, and maintain that discipline in a manner that is acceptable to your work group. Therefore you must understand what "good" discipline is and utilize it to build a productive climate in your work unit so you can maximize the results achieved by your employees.

GOOD DISCIPLINE? DOES THAT MEAN USING A SPONGE INSTEAD OF A BAT?

The best discipline is, of course, self-discipline, whereby the employee follows, voluntarily, the course he has been taught to follow, doing his share of the work and living up to the rules of the game, whatever they are. This comes naturally to most people, but it is encouraged by the existence, in the background, of clearly spelled out, reasonable rules for behavior. This type of discipline is called "positive" discipline. The rules motivate the employee to do what he is *aware* is expected with the goal of attaining a reward for this action such as security, salary considerations or promotional opportunities.

Note that the work "aware" is underlined above. It may seem obvious that such a rule is to be followed. But the employee must KNOW that there is a rule for it to be followed. The employee must UNDERSTAND that rule for it to be followed well. And, finally, the employee must see the RESULT of that rule as being positive in the overall accomplishment of the work unit goals.

When looked at in this way, the manager does not just publish the rule, expect it to be read and followed without the proper "instruction" that gives the employee understanding and motivation to follow the rule. The manager, therefore, is not pushing the work unit to succeed from behind and with a whip. The true manager is pulling the group forward by leadership and teaching so that the group can only to one thing and that is to succeed. Do you see the difference?

Therefore, your primary task is promote self-discipline and encourage employees to think positively about doing their job well because you and they know that their individual job is important to the overall success of the work unit.

BASIC IMPLEMENTATION GUIDES FOR SELF-DISCIPLINE

1. The primary principle, and it's your responsibility, is for you to establish and make sure that your employees know about and understand your policies and rules and those of the Company. It is also critical for your employees to know and understand where he and his fellow employees fit into your overall picture of the efficient running of the department.
2. Next you should, in explaining your rules and policies, show the reasons for the policy's existence in such a way that your employees UNDERSTAND and, more important, ACCEPT them.

As this chapter goes on, we will deal with methods of handling rule violations through positive intervention techniques. Be aware that discipline now means teaching not punishment. So any techniques you may learn will first center on your ability to teach as well as what you have taught to that employee. Just as in the definition, your guidelines will deal with instruction first and punishment last because future infractions will be avoided through knowledge not through punishment.

Before going on, there is one obvious step that must not be overlooked by you in maintaining good discipline. This is that you must discipline yourself before you attempt to constructively help others towards self-discipline.

Many managers believe that you should' do as I say" and "not as I do." However, in learning the process of discipline yourself, you must be in control, understand the Company's policies and rules, understand the process of the jobs under your control BEFORE you can instruct or discipline your people. There is not an employee alive who cannot spot a manager who is faking. If the manager does not know, how can he/she hold me to a standard and expect me to understand what they do not?

Interesting question, no?

The idea of "count my stripes" and if I have more than you, do what I say, is long gone. The "modern" manager has to be able to demonstrate continuously the proper work habits as well as the proper regard for the Company and its rules and regulations. When the manager fails to follow the rules, he cannot hold the employees to those rules. (You may win within the Company walls, but you will lose in court or before government agencies.)

As an example, if starting time is 8 AM and you expect your employees to be there on time, then you should be there also.

But hold on there a minute! I'm a salaried exempt employee. I don't get paid for 40 hours. Am I not entitled to a little slack when it comes to starting times, etc, since I must work until the job gets done?

In theory, the answer is yes. However, your employees do not see that as the case. In fact, the probability is that they do not understand that you are not getting paid by the hour. They will feel that you, as a manager, are "getting the big bucks" (even if that is not the case), and you can be late. Therefore, they, too, can be late. I have found that no amount of talk and logic can convince hourly employees that anyone is paid on a different basis than they are. The only difference is that you get "more."

In a recent negotiation with a union, the union contended that management was getting large, six figure salaries and did not want to share the money with them through wage increases. The facts revealed that no one in management was anywhere near six figures in salary and W-2 forms indicated that most of the negotiating committee had made more money in the previous year than 80% of the managers. Of course, the hard data could not be shared because of confidentiality. But, no amount of talk could convince the committee that this was the case. Therefore, if you are managing hourly employees, this mind set is probably the case with your people as well. Keep that in mind when you cut yourself some slack that is not available to the hourly staff.

Practice the type of leadership that other people respect and you are creating that environment for good discipline that tends, over time, to eliminate the need for "punishment" as the only definition for discipline.

QUALITY WORK IS CONFORMING TO STANDARDS. HOW DO I "DISCIPLINE" TO THAT END?

The problem of maintaining good discipline is one that varies from unit to unit, based on the personnel in the unit, their level of training, the group attitude, and, most important, the manager in charge. There is no simple pattern that, once learned, corrects all problems. Rather there is a series of ideas or suggestions that, adapted to the situation and department, aids you in establishing your own disciplinary pattern. Some of those ideas are as follows:

- Be certain that YOU know the Company, office and department rules, understand them as well as the necessity for them.
- Clearly make the rules and regulations known to your employees.
- Make sure that the instructions that you give are understood as well as why they are issued in the first place.
- Train your employees to utilize proper work methods and practices.
- Attempt to salvage the employee who is not living up to your expectations by working with him to make sure that he understands his assignment.

- Anticipate, if possible, the violation of a company rule and attempt to get the employee back on the right track before he becomes subject to punitive discipline. "Read the signs" and anticipate trouble and be honest enough to step in and prevent the infraction. Lead don't police!
- Analyze the infraction and see if all the training possible has been done for this employee as well as understanding of the process.
- After corrective action has been taken, analyze the situation to see if there is improvement or does something else need to be done.

From the standpoint of the employee, operating in a work environment, or any environment for that matter, where the sword of Damocles is always hanging over your head is not healthy nor is it beneficial to your quality work product. So train, instruct, clarify and clear the air. Then let the employee prove that he/she can do the work well. As the saying goes,"the proof is in the pudding."

What we have been talking about for the last few pages is Positive Reinforcement. This concept of corrective action has gotten some bad press over the years. To some, this concept goes against our interactive style. Let's look at what P.R. is and some objections to it.

Positive reinforcement places emphasis on praising positive results on a very systematic basis to increase performance, productivity and job satisfaction.

1. I don't have the time to tell people that they're doing a good job. I'm always dealing with those who are not performing.

   RESPONSE: If you use even a little time to reinforce positive behavior, you will probably not have to intervene on a negative basis later. Employees want you to pay attention to them. If praise for good work gets recognition, what behavior do you think employees will exhibit to you? Besides, thanking an employee for a good job is much better than taking disciplinary action for poor performance.

2. I don't think people should receive praise for just doing their jobs. Isn't that what we pay them for?

   RESPONSE: Different people are motivated by different things. We already noted this before in previous chapters. People who are doing a good job *know* that they are doing well. However, they want to know that *you* know it too. This provides the incentive for future growth in productivity through positive behavior patterns.

3. I want to be fair with everyone. I don't want to single out anyone because it may seem like I am playing favorites.

   RESPONSE: Giving praise for a job well done is not a matter of equality. A good job is a good job. Public praise should be accompanied by remarks that make it clear that the praise is for a job well done, not because of who did it. Positive reinforcement is a tool that enables you to manage your employees, help you keep the good ones, and make the average ones better. (It also makes other good employees in other departments want to work for you. So it can strengthen your entire work force.)

The attention to small detail and not accepting mediocre performance are hallmarks of success. Less than excellent performance or less than perfect service is simply not acceptable. When your employees know that they will be recognized for good performance, why would they jeopardize that recognition by performing badly? It does not follow. Therefore, the extra time spent in positive reinforcement is worth the effort in management and discipline because it lets the employee know what is ACCEPTABLE and downgrades what is not.

As an employee, which path would you normally follow?

NUTS! I'VE TRIED EVERYTHING! ALL THAT "TRAINING" HASN'T WORKED! WHAT DO I DO NOW?

Frankly, no matter how much time and effort you put into positive reinforcement or discipline, there will come a time when you have to deal with the issue in a formal manner with the attendant punishment that goes along with the problem.

There are some rules in your Company that are so serious that any violation calls for immediate dismissal or suspension. Violations such as fighting, carrying firearms, gross insubordination, etc. qualify for this type of issue. In such cases, your Company has a policy and procedure to deal with these issues. Usually, the Human Resources Department or even the Plant Manager deal directly with the employee and you, as a Manager, serve as a witness to the proceedings.

In today's environment, for these types of issues, make sure that you have all of the facts before you confront the employee and/or the union representative. Have your witness' statements, the observations from all concerned in front of you so there is no question about the violation and the consequences. Deal with this type of issue immediately BUT not before you have all of the facts. If there is a question that needs to be answered, suspend the employee(s) without pay until you have a hearing. Advise the employee(s) that they will be paid for any lost time if the alleged violation proves false or without enough proof to carry out the penalty. Set the hearing data as soon as possible AFTER you have all of the facts.

These issues are somewhat rare and you might not be involved in such a case for your entire career. But it is imperative that the issue be handled properly and legally or you will open the Company up to a severe liability in addition to having to take the employee back with back pay, even if the allegation is true but you mishandled the case. The bottom line in these cases is for you to follow the Company policy rigidly, seek advise from your boss and/or your lawyer, if necessary. It is also critical that only the right information is said to the employee, without rancor or testy or inflammatory adjectives.

Handle the issue in a professional manner with the employee and there is less danger of an escalation of feelings.

Recognize that the employee is not going to like what is happening but do not be pulled into a debate. If you have your facts, state them, the penalty and leave it at that. If a termination is involved, try to have the final check, COBRA notification papers and an explanation of any benefits that the employee might have coming. This litany tends to be a good lead into closing the meeting and sending the employee out of the meeting. It also tends to keep you from going through the wringer over and over on the same point.

When it comes to handling other issues, such as efficiency, utilization, attendance, tardiness, horse-play, etc, the Company will tend to give you a lot of leeway in dealing with the employee. It might set out penalties for infractions but it is up to you to enforce them and deal with the employee.

Unfortunately, most Companies do not train their managers on how to handle the situation so each manager develops his/her own method and they are as inconsistent as snow flakes are different. Employees search out the Manager who is the "easiest" in enforcing rules and the others are avoided because they can't get away with anything with those managers. (Human nature, huh?)

Well it behooves a Company to try to get their managers to be consistent in handling discipline that is both a positive reinforcement as well as a penalty system. In this way, all employees can be treated fairly.

WHAT SHOULD I DO?

When dealing with the non suspension or termination problems, in other words the normal day-to-day problems of management, that involve the employee's lack of understanding or continual "fouling up" in the workplace, it is important that you follow some guidelines in dealing with that employee and the situation.

First and foremost, do not deal with the situation while you are angry or upset over what has happened. Anger will cloud some good judgement and cause the manager to say things that are incorrect about the situation or personally hurtful to the employee. Why is this bad? Because your desire is to correct the problem and make sure that it doesn't happen again. If you have blinded the employee through emotion, no learning can occur. Remember the basic definition of discipline. Assuming that the offense is not a termination offense, this employee will remain on your staff and you will have to interact with him/her every day. Creating a hostile environment is not a way to create self discipline or reinforce good behavior positively because the employee will not trust you to be telling the truth about any situation.

Does this mean that I should delay any action for a period of time?

No! It is important that you deal with the situation as soon as practical. The practicality of the situation means that you have gathered ALL of the facts before having the meeting. A long delay can be a sign of weakness in that you don't want to face the employee.

It is important for you to "know" the right time. Unfortunately, this book cannot gauge that time for you.

It is never right to judge behavior based on an animal's reaction. However, when a puppy acts incorrectly with respect to "tinkling or pooping," you act immediately so the animal knows what the error in behavior really was. A delay in "punishment" will confuse the animal as to what has been done wrong.

Certainly, people are different. However, a long delay impresses on the employee that this is not a serious issue. If you land hard after this delay, the employee feels betrayed and/or confused, and rightly so.

So, act after the facts have been gathered and without emotion.

Your second guideline is that discipline should never be conducted in a public place or in front of other peers or employees. Do not make an example out of a situation for the benefit of others at the expense of one. Logically, you will never have the respect of that one and the other employees will be waiting for you to do the same thing to them. In other words, their concentration will not be on quality or continuous improvement but on waiting for the other show to fall and for you to blast them in public when that happens.

If you have to gather facts and that means asking other employees about the situation, your questions should be neutral, factual and impersonal to them and the offender.

Remember that everyone probably knows that something has gone wrong and that you are dealing with that situation. They are watching you to see how you deal with the people involved. This will enhance their respect for you or make you a totally inefficient manager in their eyes.

The third guideline deals with your meeting with the employee. The meeting should deal with the facts of the situation only. (More on this later.) What error was made and what behavior do you want changed by that employee. Frankly, it doesn't matter what you think about that employee on any personal basis. You want a quality product and that is all. Deal with the subject objectively. Do not allow the employee to make the situation personal.

Your investigation and the facts point out the situation. Then deal with the corrective action necessary to prevent this from happening again.

Finally, listen carefully to the employee's side of the issue. This will give you the insight as to whether the proper procedures and policies were fully understood as well as what you need to do to correct this errant behavior. Remember that there may be many facts in the employee's version that you have nor discovered or overlooked. This could modify your actions. If you don't listen, you could be missing something that will help your entire department.

Through active listening, understanding develops on both sides. When understanding exists, then the policies and procedures will be followed OR you will understand that some changes have to be investigated or made because they contribute to that continuous improvement.

Once a conclusion has been reached, end the meeting. Try to end the meeting on a positive note and advise that employee that the matter is closed unless the action plan that was developed is not followed. If you have done a good job with this discipline, the matter will not come up again.

By reading between the lines here, you can see that discipline is a shared responsibility.

SHARED RESPONSIBILITY? BUT I'M THE BOSS, IT'S MY JOB TO DISCIPLINE, RIGHT?

Discipline is two sided. You can shout and holler and be totally ineffective in handling your problem because there is no insight, training or instruction that the employee can understand in order to modify behavior. Remember "communication"! It takes mutual understanding of what is being said for communication to happen. You want the employee to follow the rules, don't you? Then that employee had better understand what the rules are and how you interpret them. Therefore you share that responsibility. In fact, with input from the employee, you can develop a shared action plan for corrective action that the employee not only understands but also, since he has participated in the development of the plan, will make every effort to follow carefully.

Realize that this chapter deals not only with discipline but also with positive reinforcement as a way to arrive at self discipline for all of us.

The following page sets a list of questions that you can ask yourself when you are faced with a non-conformance to rules, regulations, processes, or performance. Ask these of yourself BEFORE the disciplinary meeting. Then set your facts and call in the employee.

A. HAVE YOU DONE YOUR JOB AS MANAGER?
1. Have I clearly defined my expectations on this job?
2. Does the employee understand these expectations?

3. Is this performance part of written job standards or is there a policy statement that covers this behavior?
4. Have I provided the training necessary to the employee? or have I assumed that the employee understood?
5. Are there any major systems blockers that hinder understanding?
6. What behavior has been observed with date, time, places, witnesses?

NOW IT IS TIME TO DEAL WITH THE EMPLOYEE.

B. DID THE EMPLOYEE:
1. Acknowledge his/her behavior?
2. Specifically acknowledge the standard?
3. Acknowledge that he/she did not meet the standard?
4. Give you a specific plan as to how the standard will be met from now on?

NOW YOU MANAGE THE PERFORMANCE.

C. THE MANAGER MUST NOW:
1. Observe the employee to manage the performance.
2. If acceptable performance improvement occurs, observe it and positively reinforce it immediately.
3. If observation indicates that the employee continues to not meet the standard, intervene on the very next occurrence.

If the employee refuses to acknowledge that he/she is not meeting the standard, then you have to state the facts and witnesses who have observed this behavior and ask the employee again for their action plan to correct the behavior. Debate is not the issue. Corrective action and a plan for same is the only acceptable outcome of this intervention. Do not be led off that path by talking around the issue but never addressing it.

You must remain in control no matter what method of discipline you use. Control is maintained by being factual and not engaging in argument. The employee is not happy being in your office for this purpose. You are not happy because you have to deal with this situation. Don't allow two unhappy people to develop into a debate or, worse, a fight.

When discipline is done properly, the employee returns to the floor with an action plan clearly implanted because he/she has participated in developing the method. When the other employees ask what happened, and they will, the employee has no grounds to say that it was "personal." If truthful, the employee can only address the facts because that is all that occurred. From this, the other employees now know that, if they make an error and you call them in, they will be treated professionally and not in anger. This increases the respect within your department for your management skills.

CONCLUSION

There is no easy method for handling discipline. However, if you remember the definition as stated above, discipline does not become an adversarial situation. It is a teaching situation. This makes it easier for you and the employee.

Does one way work in every case? Unfortunately, no! Why? Because each person is different. (Do you remember that from somewhere else in this book?) Consequently, your knowledge of each individual member of your team will dictate the type of discipline that you will use to correct behavior that does not meet standards.

This individual knowledge of employees as well as their knowledge of you and your consistency and fairness in dealing with discipline is the key to your success in maintaining control over your efficiency as well as your effectiveness as a Manager in the twenty-first century.

STRESS MANAGEMENT
OR
THEY'RE DRIVING ME CRAZY!
WHAT CAN I DO?

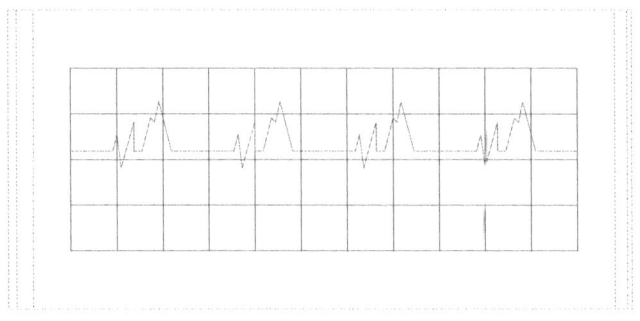

Unless our business is so easily run and our employees are perfect angels, things do not run smoothly during our work day. Most of the time, we are putting out fires and running from one project to another. The word "chaos" really has a management meaning when it comes to dealing with the day-to-day situations.

Time is short, tempers are shorter, and deadlines are impossible. Naturally, our EKG line probably does not look like the one on the left. In point of fact, the **STRESS IS KILLING ME!**

What can I do about this in my management since I recognize that this "chaos" is the norm and I will be faced with this situation throughout my career, if I last that long?

Many scholars have written tomes on this subject and many devices, both athletic and medical, have been sold to assist you to calmer waters, if you only spend the required money or visit the suggested spa. But the bottom line is that you have the power to control this problem within yourself at no cost.

This chapter will be devoted to some really simple techniques that are not magic, just logical, if you take the time to utilize them.

ACADEMIC UNDERSTANDING

Unfortunately, in order to begin, we have to begin with a definition that has some meaning. My definition is somewhat simple in that it explains the word and does not make "stress" a "four letter word."

> "Stress is any situation that makes a special demand on the body whether that demand is physiological or psychological."

Looking at that definition we can understand that "any situation" ranges from waking, eating, shaking hands, talking, making love, rocking in a chair to skydiving, bungee jumping or skin diving. If that is the case, and these activities DO place a demand on the body or mind, then "stress" can be pleasurable and desirable. Given that as a fact, how do we let ourselves get into situations where stress becomes much less than desirable?

The answer to this time honored question rests in that WE ALLOW the situation to CONTROL us and not the other way around. This will be the focus of our effort in this chapter to see this and figure how to re-gain that control.

Physiological stress is obvious. A broken arm, a run or jog that is exhausting, arthritis, or some other form of physical problem causes stress. For the purposes of this chapter, we are going to skip this side of stress and concentrate on the psychological stressors because these are the ones that tend to affect the management process more than the physical stressors.

Interaction between a manager and that manager's environment tend to produce stress, either mild or severe, depending on that situation. Small amounts of stress appear and disappear on a regular basis. However, large amount of stress may arise when the individual faces a demanding situation and is unsure of his ability to cope with the problem.

An emotion or feeling produces stress whether that emotion is love, anger, hate or joy. The anxiety caused is characterized by apprehension, tenseness, dread or foreboding. Your ability to react and control the situation will be the controller of the amount of apprehension, etc. that your body feels. Lack of control leads to frustration and, eventually, anger that may or may not be controllable.

Let's look at a "situation." If a situation exists that you must deal with today, you should determine the obstacles before making your decision. This is so you do not allow the frustration to build into anger. First, in this situation, let's say that you are a good person and that you have a need, decision, or problem that needs to be satisfied or resolved. In fact, because you are a good person, the satisfaction of that need is also good. Second, to satisfy that need, you need to overcome some obstacles, either tough or easy. Once you have determined the "toughness" of the obstacles, you can make a decision on how to satisfy your need or solve your problem. Last, accomplish your goal.

All of the above sounds easy. Yet the solution to the problem depends on the obstacles.

Some examples that I have used in the past may illustrate your dilemma. Let's say that you are in your office behind your large, wide desk. Someone comes into the room and you want to shake hands but your arms are collectively not long enough. You can struggle against the desk and become frustrated because the desk will not move or you can step back and go around the desk and shake hands. In effect, you have established control, looked at alternatives, selected one and satisfied your need. You were in control!

In another example, let us say that you are in an office that has no windows or doors and the office is made of concrete. You want to conduct some business outside your office. After many hours of trying to get through the solid walls, etc., you can do two things. One, you can get frustrated and angry or two, you can re-gain your control, realize that you will not be able to achieve your goal or satisfy your need and make a new plan on how to live within your confined office. Herein you took control, saw no alternatives to satisfying your need, and moved on with your life. Not very realistic? Let's see.

Your boss gives you a project but forbids you access to the data that you need to finish the report. How successful will your report be? What alternatives do you have? Can the obstacles be overcome? Do you feel like you're in a box? Can you get out? Do you see what is meant by frustration and anger? Is it clear how the stress would grow in this situation, if you lost control? Do you have any control at all? If not, why worry about it? In other words, some problems or positions do not have concrete solutions to those situations. Therefore do not let the situation rule you when there is no solution.

One of the most damaging stressors is the internal pressure that we place on ourselves to meet a particular standard. In fact, our own pressures are, in many cases, tougher than those imposed upon us by our management or company. Keep an eye out for the internal pressure and maintain the control that is necessary for our performance under our standards.

LIVING ON THE EDGE OR HOW TO RAISE YOUR STRESS LEVEL WITHOUT REALLY TRYING.

As you know, most of the time, we are our own worst enemies. Not only do we have the problem to solve but we also add our own complications to that solution and increase our own stress. That's not true, you say!

Many years ago I came across a list of items that were guaranteed to increase your stress. It has been too many years to remember all of the items. However, some have stuck and they are as true now as they were then.

The first item that came to mind was to be a loner and do not have a support group of any kind. Keep things to yourself and try to resolve all of your problems yourself. As you can see, such a mind set would force you to have no relationships that allow you to blow off steam; solicit new information; seek advice; or develop empathy for people. No matter how good a manager you were, this mind set keeps stress high and prevents you from being better.

Another excellent stressor is to become a workaholic and don't allow any time for rest, recreation or outside activities. This mind set leaves your thinking process so narrow that it is hard to resolve the management-type problems encountered everyday unless they fit into your pre-set pattern. In addition, the workaholic allows no activity to relieve the stress held internally in addition to the problems that are coming on a day-to-day basis. The stress continues to build up until some form of safety valve blows and produces a stroke, other physical problem or an explosion of emotion, possibly even violence. Rest assured it will come out sometime and someplace in the future if you don't vent it regularly.

Of course, not eating or sleeping on a regular basis will produce physical stress that adds to the daily grind and makes your day worse.

Remember in our earlier chapters when we spoke about self assessments of style and character to determine management capabilities. Well, in the case of stress, we have to do the self analysis so that we can re-gain control of ourselves and to determine how and where we want to go. By controlling ourselves, we control our destiny since the situation or other people are not our controllers. Redundant? Not if the message gets through. You can control your stress by taking command. If a situation is beyond your control, move on to something else.

In management this applies, as part of your responsibilities, that you control your department. Nothing in your job description says you have to control yourself. However, success will be determined by your ability to control your stressors so you can perform the activities that are listed in your job description.

TECHNIQUES FOR STRESS CONTROL AND RELAXATION

There are many techniques, some very expensive, to assist one in reducing stressors. You can find these advertised in abundance. All of them say they have the real answer to your stress reduction. Just try them and you'll see. (Probably at some not so nominal cost, too.)

In this book, however, I am going to reveal to you the REAL MAGIC METHOD of controlling your stress. The method is complicated so you will have to pay close attention. Since it involves two elements, this complication grows even more radically. So pay careful attention.

The first element requires you to tense your muscles, as if you were flexing. The second complicated element is breathing. Yes, that is correct! You now have the keys to stress reduction and it didn't cost you a thing. How does this work?

If you had studied a form of martial arts, the philosophy not the physical, you found that muscle control and proper breathing can accomplish marvelous, refreshing renewal to the body and mind. The method is to take a deep breath, hold it while tensing your muscles. Then exhale slowly while slowly relaxing your muscles. By the time you have exhaled completely, your muscles should be totally relaxed. This relaxation method works well after a little practice.

Before going further, the breathing element is a little more complicated than just taking a breath. Were you aware that most of us do not breath properly?

Take a deep breath and watch yourself in the mirror! Observe that most of us raise our shoulders up while we breath in; we also expand our upper body. While this looks good, it does not allow our lungs to get a full complement of air. In fact, scientists advise that we tend to only get half of the air needed by our normal breathing.

Given the above, how should I breathe? When a deep breath is taken, inhale and fill your stomach with air. (Your stomach should expand as the air is going in. This will double the volume of air intake.) No, it does not look good but it allows you twice the air capacity and potential stress reduction. Of course, you can use your stomach muscles as a bellows for the exhaling process so the muscles gain strength and you maintain your physique.

By combining the tensing and breathing elements into a rhythm of breathing, tensing, exhaling, and relaxing, you can , within seconds, regain the control over your body that you need and want.

What is the magic of this method? Frankly, there is none. What happens by tensing is that you restrict the flow of blood through your veins. The deep exhalation of breath forces air out, allows the heart to bump fully and all of that fresh oxygen to enrich your blood while your veins open up. Since much of our tension and stressors cause restricted blood vessels, this method opens the vein pathways and relieves that tension. Incidently, this method can be done anytime and anywhere, even in the management meetings or grievance hearings. By controlling your own stressors, you are in a better position to control the events of the day, without anyone else knowing what you are doing.

The above method is a "quick fix" for the problems. What can you do for yourself if you have more time?

Using the same technique of tensing and breathing, you can perform a progressive relaxation exercise that also leads to tranquility.

Start by sitting upright in a comfortable chair, placing your feet flat on the floor. Rest your arms by your side and close your eyes. Then the exercise begins:

1. Tense your feet and take a deep breath. Slowly relax your feet and exhale.
2. Tense your lower legs and take a deep breath. Slowly relax and exhale. (Feel the tension leave your legs as you relax.)
3. Tense your thighs and take a deep breath. Slowly relax and exhale.
4. Tense your posterior and take a deep breath. Slowly relax and exhale.
5. Make fists and take a deep breath. Slowly relax and exhale.
6. Tense your forearms and take a deep breath. Slowly relax and exhale.
7. Tense your upper arms and take a deep breath. Slowly relax and exhale.
8. Tense your shoulders and take a deep breath. Slowly relax and exhale.
9. Tense your neck and take a deep breath. Slowly relax and exhale.
10. Continue to take deep breaths and exhale slowly.

It is important that you concentrate on each part of the body that is tensing and breathe in rhythm with the tensing and relaxing of the muscles. As you progress through your body, each part of your system will relax more and more. When you have moved up through the neck and continue deep breathing, your body should be completely relaxed and your mind free from stress.

Again, there is no magic with this method. It is a form of self hypnosis. The absolutely worse thing that can happen to you in this state is that you fall asleep. Since this method is designed for complete relaxation, falling asleep is not a bad thing. In addition, many of us have a tendency to wake in the middle of the night and our minds race on and on about the day's problems or tomorrow's difficulties. Probably, we cannot get back to sleep no matter how hard we try. If you try this method of relaxation, you should be able to go back to sleep within a short time and your mind will be relaxed.

Why does this work? Simply because you are concentrating on yourself, on your body, on your breathing. You are taking control of you! Since you are now in command, you can direct your body and mind as you see fit.

Remain in control of yourself and you can control the situations around you and manage accordingly.

COPING

Now we get to the nitty gritty. I understand what has been said and that's great. But how do I handle myself with all of these stressors hitting me along with the normal management problems that arise every day?

Effective coping involves learning to use socially acceptable methods that can 1) reduce the impact of stress; 2) alter the environment to reduce the amount of stress; 3) change one's own behavior so that less stress will be experienced. We tend to learn to use these strategies at birth and is characterized by our own personality. Mental health, then, is related to man's ability to adjust to his environment and to other people.

Direct or active coping is action oriented—consciously taking action to alter uncomfortable stress provoking situations. The source of the stress must be consciously recognized before this can happen. If the situation produces extreme hopelessness, action can only be taken to try to control the effects. (Remember the person in the concrete room with no windows or doors?) The bottom line is that some of the most effective action might be to withdraw and/or flee the situation. (The old fight or flight concept.)

Action, action, action! To act means to do something. To do something you must control.

If you can control yourself, you can control your stress and take any appropriate actions required for any situation.

Stress needs to be managed and your success or failure will depend on your ability to handle yourself and your employees through their stressful situations and environments as well as your own.

Don't talk about it, DO IT!

NOW THAT I KNOW ME AND MY EMPLOYEES, HOW DO I PUT THEM TOGETHER AS A TEAM?

As you have determined during your self-examination as well as your review of your employees, each person is different and, as such, is motivated by a wide variety of factors. These motivators range from money to security to self esteem to the work itself. You recognize that, in order for you to succeed, you have to produce a product or service that assists the Company to achieve a profit. To do this, your people must work together and act as a TEAM.

But with all of this diversity, how can that be done?

In the April issue of the Harvard Business Review, Jon Katzenbach and Douglas Smith wrote an excellent article on *THE DISCIPLINE OF TEAMS*. They define a team as a "small number of people with complementary skills who are committed to a common purpose, set of performance goals and approach for which they hold themselves mutually accountable." Contained in this definition are many variable factors that take us back to the beginning of this book and identify again the need for self examination as well as examination of the motivators of our employees.

Before this gets too psychological, let's put the team members in perspective.

First, we have already examined our own and our employee's thought process. Who you are and what you want to do is clear in your mind. Is this the same process that is in the mind of your employees?

Second, let us not confuse a relationship concept that we must "like each other" in order to be a team. This is not so. In fact, team members who know their jobs well and can be led to the common goal, are more effective than a group of people whose feelings for each other are the sole motivators of their success.

In addition, do not confuse good relations with approval. One can "approve" what is established as the goal and not "like" the leader and visa versa. Therefore approval has value only when it is a motivator toward the common goal.

Some feel that the relationship is good if we don't disagree. Not so! While the goal may be worthwhile and acceptable, the road to achievement may have many turns and forks. Selection of the appropriate turn can and should lead to disagreement so the best choice may be made by the leader.

Third, dealing with the differences of opinion, personality, and humanity will dictate the success or failure of that team. Is there a balance between reason and emotion among the members of the team? Is there understanding of the goal and good communications among the group? Are the members of the group reliable? Is there a mutual acceptance of the skills of the individuals to perform their individual assignments well?

Finally, reason must prevail. However, too much emotion clouds judgement because of the individual's bias and too little impairs motivation and understanding. Whether you view Aristotle's definition of reason or that of Jung, the bottom line is that you have to maintain that thread of reason that leads toward the goal that has been established. Using the symphony, you can see that the conductor cannot let the violin section or the trumpet section dominate the flutes or the oboes. The conductor selects the best qualities of each and plays them up or down based on the goal being achieved. This is true in your decision making process. Use the skills available, motivating and leading the players toward your goal. This element is basic in team building.

Getting back to the above definition, how many constitute a "small group"?

Anthropologists tell us that the cavemen moved in groups of ten. Each person had a specific assignment, that of hunter, wise man, cook, fire carrier, wood gatherer, etc. This collection of skills were established over time for the very survival of the group. While the number (10) might vary, up or down, the establishment of skills for survival or goal achievement for the group does not vary. Too many in the group and people are falling over each other. Too few and some of the skills needed are absent. In both cases, the goal is not achieved.

Therefore we might say that the number is controlled by the number of NECESSARY skills needed to achieve the goal. The military uses fire teams, squads, platoons, companies, etc to build their organizations. Business leaders use the same concept to build the corporation from the section to department to division, etc. Both concepts utilize the economy of scale. What are the fewest number of skills that I need to reach my goal? In business, this is called controlling your burden, labor variance, and cost. Through this, maximum profit can be achieved and your success assured.

The next part of the definition deals with "complementary skills." In the selection of the skills necessary you need a variety of skills that will help the group to work toward the goal. If digging a ditch, you need people with shovels not a tool and die maker. That skill might be great to have but it is not necessary to achieve the group's goal. Having that right blend of skills is what makes them "complementary."

The most significant part of this definition is that this is a group "who is committed to a common purpose." Herein in where all of the work you have done to know your people and their skills comes into play. If you can get each of your people to work toward the common goal, you will have mastered the team building skill. No where in the definition does it say "group of people who like each other." Nor does it say "group of people who hang out with each other." It just says "group of people who work toward a common purpose." In other words, don't try to force a relationship based on emotion. Base the relationship on appreciation for each individual skill that helps everyone to achieve their goal.

The last part of this definition is the toughest to get across to employees. That is that everyone is "accountable" for their production and their skill level. In order for a team to succeed, each person must perform. Efficiency and utilization are both individual and group entities. You can make the rate but only work half the time on direct labor and not achieve the production goal. This is a disaster for your team. Employees tend to not want to be accountable because it is too clear a measure of success or failure. Your team needs to know that you are not the only "accountable" person on the team. In fact, a close reading of the definition shows that the "accountability" is to the group. Each employee is accountable to each and every member of the team for the successful performance of their skill. Certainly, if applied properly, this concept makes your job as manager much easier because all of the employees are pointed to the goal and ALL are to use their skills to the best of their ability OR they have to answer to their fellow team members. While this makes complete sense, it is a hard message to get across. For the twenty-first century, as well as for now, the team concept makes us "lean and mean" in the corporate environment because we are producing the quality product or service at the lowest cost at the greatest efficiency.

Your job in team building? Put all of the elements together so that they fit. Assess the skills available, modify them, add to them or change them so they complement each other. Place people on the team with the applicable skills and focus them on the common goal. If the people have the skill and accept the goal, then you are on your way to a successful team and the achievement of the common goal.

In conclusion, Katzenbach and Smith state that management "must recognize a team's unique potential to deliver results, deploy teams strategically when they are the best tool for the job, and foster the basic discipline of teams that will make them effective. By doing so, management creates the kind of environment that enables team as well as individual and organizational performance."

Once the environment is created, it is up to you to develop the team through reason, emotion, and skill level needed. Once done, your team, if focused on a common goal, produces the result to make you and them successful.

Building the team brings full circle the definition of management, that is "getting the job done, through people." The concept of "through people" and your ability to develop that team will make or break you as a manager in the twentieth or the twenty-first century.

**HERE YOU ARE!
AT THE TOP OF THE HEAP!
THE BOSS!
IT'S TOUGH TO GET THERE!
CAN YOU STAY?**

The entire focus of this book has been on priming a manager for the twenty-first century. However, if you had read carefully, you noticed that the contents apply to experienced and new managers; to this century, the last century *and the next century*.

Most of the items already mentioned deal with gaining and developing a managerial perspective. Understanding of the Company's goals and objectives as opposed to personal objectives leads us to that perspective where we can focus on team building and common, achievable goals that will lead to your success.

The balance that is reached, as a Manager, is to determine how to make decisions and set expectations that will *simultaneously* satisfy the requirements of all parties involved—the workers, the Company, the manager, and, most important, the customer.

We have not mentioned this last element too often. However, we understand that without that customer the Company ceases to exist. Even if you are the best manager in the universe, if there is nothing to produce then you have no job.

Let's summarize our managerial perspective:

- *Learn everything there is to know about yourself.* Examine your attitudes, characteristics, and personality so you can utilize ALL of your strengths; develop your weaknesses; and become a whole person when dealing with your employees.

- *Take the time to develop yourself.* Many feel that it is selfish to concentrate on oneself. Taken to an extreme, it might be. However, a complete knowledge of your weaknesses allows you to work on them and improve them. If the weaknesses cannot be overcome, you might not be able to be a good manager. But understanding them, helps you to maintain the control necessary for development.
- *Look deeply at each member of your staff.* Concentrate on their personalities, skills, families, motivators, and goals. Utilize those skills that are presented and develop new ones based upon your knowledge of that individual. Understand the individual so you can build the staff and steer it toward the common goal.
- *Understand what you are asked to do.* When you are required to make a product or perform a service, determine what factors are involved in the manufacture or performance before you ask others to do the work. See what skills are required. Do your people have the basic skills to do the work? Take action to see that your final staffing DOES have the requisite skills.
- *Believe that discipline is a training program.* Follow the guidelines that the Company establishes and make sure that your employees know and understand those same guidelines. Only when the training component fails to produce the desired result would you engage in a punitive progressive discipline.
- *Establish your team based on skill and focus them on a common goal.* Using the symphony conductor as an illustration, your job is to make all of the diverse skills work in harmony and produce the "sound" that is pleasing to the Company.
- *Recognize that you must control yourself, emotionally and physically.* The increases in your stress level can be geometric is you do not establish your control.

Determine if you will stand and face the issue or put it aside (Fight or Flee). If you stand and fight, control your environment and body through deep breathing and relaxation techniques applied during the crisis. Do not wait until after it is over to begin. After the crisis is over, apply the longer relaxation techniques that are designed to give you deep rest.

A primer is designed to be a beginning. Obviously, much more could have been written about each subject. However, the intent was to provide a "handbook for survival" that applies to all industries and management personnel. Like the union contract, keep this book in your pocket and make reference to it as you meet your daily crises. Hints about handling those crises are contained herein.

The more you use it, the less you need carry it around. The more you use it, the more information you should seek from other books, periodicals, professional journals, and industry newspapers. Hopefully, this book was written in the vernacular (English) and without the ponderance of academia. It is a book designed for the pocket and not the reference shelf.

Aristotle in words spoken by Socrates once said;

"That man is wisest who knows that he does not know."

Since this is the beginning, read, absorb and use any and every bit of information that will lead to your success as well as the growth of that success.

Never assume that since you are a Manager you are complete. The title means that you have begun a journey over terrain covered with boulders, rivers and cliffs. Keep your eyes open, learn and DO!

Ben Franklin said it all:

"WELL DONE" IS BETTER THAN "WELL SAID"!

BIBLIOGRAPHY

HARVARD BUSINESS REVIEW,
Various authors, Quarterly publication.
> Excellent review of articles, some are even in English, on management issues. Helps understand trends in management as well as review new and old ideasby some of the gurus of the process, some academic and some practical.

BOOKS BY PETER DRUCKER,
Any that you can find.
> Mr. Drucker has penned many books over the years on a wide range of management topics, any or all will give the manager a good grounding in practical management.

THRIVING ON CHAOS,
Tom Peters
> Mr. Peters' books have centered on obtaining excellence through outstanding customer service. However, this book derives as a premise that management operates in a chaotic environment and the successful manager will be the one who is able to change, moderate, and motivate customers and employees who are also living in this chaotic environment.

MANAGEMENT TIME: WHO'S GOT THE MONKEY?
Oneken and Wass, HBR, November-December Issue, 1974
> *A must-read article on managers who try to do everyone's job as well as his/her own and how the employee shifts the responsibility from their shoulders to yours. If you read nothing else, READ THIS.*

LEADER TO LEADER,
Hesselbein & Cohen, Jossey-Bass Publishers
> *Leadership ideas and insights from the Drucker Foundation*

ABOUT THE AUTHOR

Joseph L. Dineen

Joseph Dineen received his BA from Fordham University in New York and his MBA and PhD from St. John's University in Louisiana, concentrating in Business, Human Resources and Counseling. His background includes management in the fields of human resources, customer service, technical service, legal compliance, and general/executive management in several fields.

Married with two children and four grandchildren, Mr. Dineen resides in South Carolina.